D1192639

I Learn Better By Teaching Myself

Agnes Leistico

I Learn Better By Teaching Myself
Agnes Leistico

Home Education Press
Post Office Box 1083
Tonasket, WA 98855
(509) 486-1351

First Printing: March, 1990
Second Printing: September, 1991
Third Printing: October, 1992
Fourth Printing with minor revisions: April, 1994

ISBN 0-945097-10-7

Library of Congress Cataloging-in-Publication Data

Leistico, Agnes
    I Learn Better By Teaching Myself / Agnes Leistico
        p. cm.
Includes biographical references.

ISBN 0-945097-10-7   : $9.75
1. Home schooling. 2. Education-Parent participation.
1. Title.
LC40.L45   1990
649.48-dc20   90-31319
                                   CIP

TABLE OF CONTENTS

Lovingly dedicated to my husband Dale
and the children who brought about our
family's learning adventures: James, Laurene,
and Susan.

"I like to learn by teaching myself. I don't
like someone else to teach me because I learn
better by teaching myself."

Susan Leistico, age seven

FOREWORD

Have your ever considered yourself a home schooling expert? Perhaps you have, but if you're like most parents, it's more likely that you've never really thought of yourself as an expert in the field. You teach your children, or you nudge them in the directions you think might be best for them, or you let them learn as they need and want to, and you hope for the best. You have days when everything goes well and great wonderful discoveries are made and learning is obviously taking place... and then you have days when everything drags along and nothing "academic" seems to happen, and you find yourself wondering if it's all going to work out.

That might not be the generally accepted description of an expert, but when it comes to home schooling your own children - how they learn best, and what they need most - you are the only *real* expert. It doesn't matter if you are just imagining what home schooling could do for your family or if you have been doing it for years - you are still the expert.

Other peoples' titles of "home schooling expert" are based on their own experiences with whatever parenting or training or reading or studying they may have done. You can base your expert title on the very same things, but with a specialty in your own family. This is an expert title that no one else can earn. You have lived with this youngster from his or her birth, and grown as a parent as your child has grown as a person. You've shared many experiences that make your insight uniquely valuable for your child's future. The people who are often considered the "experts" have plenty of valid information for you to select from and use, but their information must be filtered through this special expertise you have as a parent.

Home schooling experts write books, teach workshops, develop curriculums, edit newsletters, lead seminars, testify in court, organize conventions, and even publish magazines. These people have valuable information to share with people who are interested in teaching their own children. In writing, teaching, publishing, testifying and organizing they are demonstrating faith in *your* ability to be the real expert your family needs. And these people offer such a wide variety of options to choose from that it can be frustrating to select the "best" for your family.

Just how do you, as your family's expert, choose a book or a curriculum or a workshop from the ever-increasing choices available? How does one sort through the "home schooling experts" and their offerings to find those which might be right for your family, and your approach to home schooling? The first step is to trust in your ability to be the *real* expert. You can start by determining your family's philosophy or motivation for home schooling. Examine your reasons for wanting to teach your own children at home, and list the methods your family feels comfortable with. Explore the subject, ask each other questions, discuss why you're home schooling, how it's working, and what changes various family members might like to see incorporated.

Knowing the approaches and methods that your family prefers will help when confronted with the wondrous selection of resources available at a curriculum fair, a home schooling conference exhibit hall, or through a home school supplier's catalog. Realizing what your family would like to work on will help in selecting workshops or seminars to attend, or in deciding which home schooling books to purchase. Envisioning the goals your family would like to achieve will make choosing the routes to those goals a fun and rewarding adventure for everyone.

As the Home Schooling Expert in your family, your decisions and selections will determine the direction and the ultimate consequences of your endeavors. Trust your abilities, believe in your own expertise, and then see what the "other experts" have to offer!

Mark and Helen Hegener
Publishers
Home Education Press

INTRODUCTION

Why do we allow adults greater freedom to learn according to individual learning styles than our children? More importantly, why don't we adults trust children to learn according to their personal interests? Could it be we turn many of today's American children away from learning long before they attain adulthood because we do not allow our children the freedom of choice in utilizing their personal learning styles? These questions have puzzled me. I realize there can be no easy answer. I take comfort in the knowledge that many noted educators also ask these questions and seek answers.

How can we encourage our children more effectively in their learning experiences? There is a widespread recognition that each person has a particular learning style that maximizes the quest for learning. This search for effective educational methods leads us to consider earlier proponents of various learning styles.

The noted author, educator, and home school pioneer John Holt advocated allowing children greater freedom in choosing what to learn when they were ready. Observing how young children learn to walk, to talk, and to function in social settings, he reasoned that this was a natural process and that later learning should flow just as naturally. Based on this he argued that learning involves the whole being of the learner. When self-esteem is left intact the child can wisely choose what learning is important and how to acquire it.

He is not alone in believing that children are the best judges of what should be learned, when it should be learned, and how it should be learned. Other noted educators have come to the same conclusion. Each has approached the question from different angles because each has had different backgrounds and insights and each approaches learning in varying ways. Maria Montessori emphasized the early childhood years and the respect for each young learner as an individual. Judson Jerome compared learning to gardening in which learning emerges when interference is avoided, nutrients are supplied, and pests are combatted.

Among other advocates of student directed learning experiences is Herbert Kohl, who addressed the need to consider the interests of the child for effective learning in his book, The Open Classroom. In Deschooling Society Ivan Illich contends that our society is inclined to believe the only valuable skills are those which are the result of formal schooling. Repeatedly we hear of educators and those vitally interested in education who state that the well-motivated or interested student usually needs no more assistance than that someone demonstrates on demand how to do what the student wants to learn to do. Students learn when they are interested in the subject.

Helen K. Billings, the founder of the Montessori Institute of America, devoted her life to promoting the concept that learning starts in early childhood and continues throughout a person's lifetime. She emphasized that student initiated learning is the foundation for true education. She especially cautions adults to wait until invited into a student's activities as the learner's interest can wane at any semblance of pressure.

Carl Rogers came to the conclusion only self-discovered, self-appropriated learning influences behavior. Noted author and educator David Elkind pleads for consideration of what he terms healthy education. His focus is on how a healthy education supports and encourages spontaneous learning processes. In his view miseducation ignores the necessity of letting young students explore and understand their immediate world. Attempting to teach the wrong thing at the wrong time causes a loss of the positive attitude a student needs for learning. He joins many others in stating that it is important not to introduce information before the student shows an interest. The list of people advocating student directed learning is long. Each has his or her variation of the theme that student initiated learning is the most effective means of learning.

For purposes of this book the definition of interest initiated learning will be that learning which the learner herself controls and initiates according to her own interests. Internal personal priorities guide her learning. Being entirely self directed, the learner chooses when and how to learn about a given topic or skill. The teacher only enters into the learning process when invited to do so.

There are many books available now about home schooling - what it is, how to start home schooling, why people home school, and the legal implications of home schooling - yet I have not heard of any which address how parents implement interest initiated learning. This book attempts to fill this gap by showing the reader how our family tries to practice interest initiated learning.

Our family is far from perfect. We have our good days mixed in with our bad days and we only imperfectly employ the concept of interest initiated learning. My hope is that it will encourage those readers already accepting the idea to continue their own efforts to reach this ideal. And may those readers who oppose the idea of interest initiated learning begin to understand what we are doing. I myself had to struggle with my own resistance to the idea that a student can learn without being told what and how to learn. My own children forced me to reconsider.

This book will present not only our story, but glimpses of how and why other families are practicing interest initiated learning. Each family needs to approach interest initiated learning in its own way as we are dealing with individual students in circumstances not duplicated in any other family. Take from this book what applies to your circumstances. Build on ideas presented to suit your family's needs. Above all, trust your own instincts.

There are three basic aspects to interest initiated

learning as brought forth in this book. One - it is that learning which the learner herself initiates and controls according to her own interests. Two - her own priorities (not imposed from the outside) guide the learner. And three - the teacher only enters into the process when invited to do so.

I do not claim to have many answers about why what is happening works, I just know it is working well for us. Our experiences and results will not be the same as another family's. In preparation for this book I have come more fully to the conclusion that the individual student/learner does know what is best for her. Too many of our students never have the opportunity to come to this realization. There are many theories and methods around. Each person has to study them and choose what works best. There is no single approach that works for everybody.

If all I do is instill in my youngsters a lifelong love for learning, I will have accomplished my goal. I firmly believe that interest initiated learning is a means to this goal for us.

Agnes Leistico

CHAPTER ONE

GETTING STARTED

In 1983 I met my first home school family. The mother and I were La Leche League leaders. We lived over 200 miles apart and were involved in a joint activity which required us to meet at each others' homes periodically. Up until that time I had never heard of home schooling and from what I saw I was not at all impressed because the youngsters *seemed* to be doing nothing. "Schooling" meant blackboards, texts, worksheets, schedules, tests, and a certain amount of boredom to me at that time. These children always seemed to be reading something or doing some "foreign" activities the limited time I was around them.

This mother had secondary teaching credentials yet did not seem in the least worried that her youngsters weren't learning anything in my estimation. She tried answering my questions but we were on different wavelengths. While I accepted the fact that she was entitled to her own point of view, I was convinced she was harming her childrens' chances in later life to be successful and accepted.

Then when I learned that a friend living nearby had also begun home schooling her son and daughter, I actively started resisting the idea. This was too much for me. I had great respect for both mothers but I could not accept their choice of education for their children. When two good friends of mine declared they were going to home school their little ones, I began to investigate why families choose to home school. But I was only willing to allow this in the case of little children. My own children were doing well in the local public schools. I felt that if parents were actively involved in their children's schools problems could be worked out.

The first two families had older children and they were practicing what I now refer to as interest initiated learning. However, my friends Linda and Christine had children younger than mine who had never gone to school at all and they were following a curriculum more traditionally oriented under the auspices of a private school. This I could more easily accept at this stage.

In June of 1985 another friend organized a workshop on home schooling. I would not consider home schooling personally but I realized this was a movement in which several of my friends were interested. I felt I should learn as much as I could about the movement in order that I might better understand home schooling.

A month later I attended the La Leche International conference in Washington, D.C., where I attended a session on home schooling. I discovered the far reaching effects of the movement and that friends I had made in the La Leche League in both the U. S. and in Canada were now home schooling. I began to realize there were numerous approaches to learning at home although most tended to be very loosely structured as opposed to what took place in my childrens' public school classes. In spite of all this exposure I was still convinced my youngsters were doing fine where they were.

Our oldest child, Jim, was reluctant to attend school in the third grade. When he was in kindergarten he could hardly wait to get to school each morning and cried when there was a holiday as he wanted to go to school. By second grade his enthusiasm had waned but I noticed no special problems. I thought he liked his third grade teacher. But there were so many days he complained of a headache or would say he did not feel well so that he would not have to go to school. Our doctor and the teacher both advised us to make him go unless Jim had a fever or some obvious symptom.

I felt this was wrong but many times ended up driving a very unhappy son to school. We lived within walking distance but sometimes the only way I could get him to go to school was to drive him. This led to more tears. Many times I allowed him to stay home but I was torn inside. My instincts told me it was a mistake to force him, yet "experts" were telling me I'd regret it later on if I did not make him go to school. As things turned out I have regretted forcing him go and have never regretted keeping him at home.

Fourth grade found a somewhat happier student although we still had days when he preferred to stay home. That year I allowed him to stay home without much fuss. Fifth grade seemed even better. There were some signs of stress which I chose to ignore as they appeared much less frequently. The one disturbing thing that occurred was that Jim started saying he did not like science. His teacher was science oriented. From what I could observe as a parent volunteer working in the classroom, the teacher was offering students a fascinating introduction to science. To this day Jim declares a dislike for science. Yet if you present him with a topic and don't label it "science," he enthusiastically digs right in.

Sixth grade was a disaster. our district takes sixth graders from the neighborhood elementary school and places them with seventh and eighth graders on a separate campus. They now have a six period day and move from classroom to classroom. Sixth graders were given a core teacher for three of their classes so they would not have to adjust to as many teachers.

Jim was miserable. Some of his teachers recognized this and tried to help us work out the problem. One teacher requested a counselor to see Jim in November. We later learned that it is not uncommon for some students to react negatively to the middle school. But because Jim was not a behavior problem, the counselor did not see him until January when the teacher had to send him to the counselor's office as he was so miserable.

Jim went into therapy. By mid February I decided he had to be home schooled. The therapist did everything she could to dissuade me from bringing Jim home to do his studies. Yet she recommended that Jim had to be removed from the middle school even though there were no suitable alternatives to the middle school in Jim's case. (Within six months she had admitted the wisdom of bringing Jim home.)

I called the school district office to check into an independent study program. There was none available. I was referred to the County Schools office. When I told the woman I was looking into an independent study program for my sixth grade son her first question was "Who's your son's probation officer?" This floored me! I explained that he was not in trouble with the law. He was a straight A student well liked by every one of his teachers, and just needed an alternative learning situation. She had nothing to offer me.

This forced me into seriously considering home schooling. Linda lent me all the back issues of *Growing Without Schooling*, John Holt's bimonthly newsletter for people interested in home schooling. It took several days of constant reading, but I read every page searching for anything that would apply to older students. There was very little written then about working with older students so I had to rely on my instincts and whoever I could find to encourage me.

The local children's librarian at our public library was an enormous help. Pat was a retired teacher with an intense love for children and great understanding of the gifted child. Together we learned more about home schooling. She was able to purchase appropriate books for the library on related topics. She encouraged us and was helpful in locating reading material in which Jim was interested.

A few months before we removed Jim from middle school I had learned that another friend had chosen to start home schooling her ten year old daughter and five year old son. This amazed me as I never dreamed Karen would do anything that "drastic." Her husband was provost of the College of Creative Studies at the University of California at Santa Barbara. She just did not seem the type to me. Yes, I was guilty of stereotyping.

I knew that Karen was using the same home school organization as Linda and Christine so I wanted to look over her daughter's fifth grade materials. Besides, my husband was not at all convinced this would work. One evening we went over to their house to talk with them and to listen to Max's thoughts about his children learning at home and how he felt this would affect their chances to go to college. He told us of the Young Scholar's program offered at the College of Creative Studies for gifted children as early as seventh grade, urging us to consider the math program for Jim.

Because I had grave personal misgivings as to my ability to direct my childrens' studies, we chose to go with the same home school organization with which my friends were enrolled. This bought time for Jim. We enrolled him immediately, but it took a few weeks to gather the materials and to be assigned a teacher, and his only contact with the teacher was through the mail.

Jim needed the time he could get just to get in touch with himself once again. For about six months he would not pick up a book to read even for enjoyment unless he was directed to. His teacher was sympathetic and demanded only the minimum. He spent most of his days outside in our yard gardening and soaking up sun. I was quite involved as a parent volunteer in the two schools his sisters were attending so was not home for stretches of time each day. This turned out to be what he needed - time to be by himself for at least part of the day.

I wrote to a home schooling friend living in Indiana. Pam had been home schooling for four years. *"I desperately need to talk to someone doing it with teenagers to see how it works. Everyone I have met or known up to now have younger children. I did try to call you last weekend when I especially felt the need to talk to you about teenagers and home schooling, but no one answered.*

"Jim is doing nicely now that the pressure is off him. He gets along with Laurie again like he used to - what a blessing. And his intense emotional reactions have calmed down considerably. Last week he even went to the Outdoor School of Santa Barbara

County Schools for a week of Science Camp offered for sixth graders. He had already paid for the trip last December but we did not know if he would actually go as the entire group is made up of students he knew from Middle School. But he did and came home tired but pleased with himself. It was a marvelous experience."

Pam's reassuring reply came promptly. *"In addition to his paper route and Kung Fu, Tim (15) is taking a continuing education class at Purdue Calumet. The class is a private pilot ground school class. He's also doing volunteer work in the summer reading program at the library (part of the graduation requirements for Clonlara - volunteer work). The topper was he got a paying (real $!) job at the county swimming pool and works there four days a week. Yes, a home schooling student can earn real money!*

"I tell you all this about Tim not only to let you know how crazy we are but to assure you (and myself sometimes) that home schooling teens are 'normal'. The first year is really rough, Agnes, at least it was for me. I was so afraid they wouldn't continue to learn, but would forget everything they had previously learned - as if we always retain everything presented to us."

In the meantime I continued reading everything I could find about home schooling methods. The more I read and talked with people, the more I realized the value of interest initiated learning. My confidence increased.

Because of important disagreements in philosophy with the organization Jim had been enrolled in, I chose to take full responsibility for his education. I came to view education as a life experience that cannot be confined by time or textbook. I wanted Jim to know he got credit for every meaningful experience - something he had not been given before. In theory I was still resisting the concept of interest initiated learning, but in practice I was gradually accepting it.

It was only after I had been working with my youngsters at home for some time that I began to realize how my own background contributed to this educational endeavor. Learning has always played an important part in my life as a source of enjoyment and fulfillment. As Jim, Laurie and Susan came along I passed this on to them without realizing it until someone called it to my attention.

Growing up in a rural community, I attended one room Highland School, where total enrollment for all eight grades never exceeded 20 students while I attended it. My father had attended the same school and for the first three years I had the same teacher he'd had. In the seventh grade four one room schools in our mountainous district consolidated into a four room school - still with an enrollment of less than 100 students.

It was quite an event to have to ride the bus to town to a high school with over a thousand students. Yet our little one room schoolhouse produced an unusual number of honor students in high school. I remember one neighbor asking why this was so. Over the years little Highland School had produced several valedictorians. I attribute this to the positive learning experience we had in our little one room school.

My grandfather had little formal education as he had grown up in a rural area of Missouri in the late 1800's. He had to devote most of his childhood to helping the family survive. In the early 1900's he came to California to establish his own large farm holdings. By the time my dad was born Highland School was established and he attended it on a regular basis. He was able to complete little more than a year of high school when his father became gravely ill and was not expected to live long. There were several sisters and a younger brother to care for so my dad had to take over the ranch as a teenager.

Grandpa lived many more years. I was an adult when he died in his mid nineties. My impression of him to this day remains one of a man very much in tune with the world around him. He always had books and magazines around, and I often saw him reading. I loved to be around him.

My own father also reads extensively. He is a craftsman known for his innovative way of making tools fit a need or purpose. My mother was a registered nurse. She too is an avid reader. My brothers and I grew up in an atmosphere that encouraged learning all we could. My husband's father, too, had to leave formal schooling after the eighth grade. Yet he can hold his own with most people who have had a college education. The common thread between my father and my father-in-law is their desire to learn as much as possible and their love of reading a variety of materials.

My college years led me into teaching. But when I started teaching I was dismayed to discover that my students resisted my efforts to make them learn. The "methods" I had been taught just did not seem to work. Youngsters did not *want* to learn what I was teaching them. Yet when I worked with adults who came of their own choice I had a different experience. I found working with them enjoyable. Something was not working right with the youngsters so I gave up teaching them altogether.

When we were married I knew that I wanted to be at home with my children as they grew up. I joined La Leche League before Jim was born and soon became a La Leche League leader. As a leader I had to become knowledgeable as to all aspects of breastfeeding and to lead discussion meetings on breastfeeding and parenting topics. At last I had found my niche.

However I did not equate my work as a La Leche leader with my teaching efforts until just recently. Now I can see the relationship. These women came to the meetings because they had the desire to learn as much as they could about breastfeeding and parenting. They expected me to be a resource person and a guide but they did not want to be spoon-fed the information.

I led the meetings with the expectation that these were intelligent women who were interested in the topic and capable of drawing their own conclusions. They were free to come to the meetings when they wanted and when it met their needs. They knew I would accept them as individuals who would be making their own decisions as to the worth of my information to them. Now I ask myself why we can't allow our children the same freedom to acquire knowledge.

As Jim, Laurie and Susan grew from babyhood to toddlerhood I just did what came naturally - which was to let them explore the world on their own terms. I tried to provide as many exploratory opportunities as possible. None of this was done with conscious thought as to its learning value.

My husband commented when Jim was about ten as to how comfortable the children were with using the library. His comment surprised me at the time because I had not deliberately set out to make them love the library. I love books so I am drawn to any library. This introduced Jim, Laurie and Susan to them. Each child could hardly wait for the time the library allowed them to have their own card. It is because the youngsters love going to the library that my husband has started making use of it himself. We have been fortunate to live near a library that has a good story time program for preschoolers. We surrounded ourselves with books we enjoyed with no particular thought as to educational value. Even before he learned to read, Jim would often fall asleep with a book in his hands. He still does occasionally. In fact, we all read before going to sleep almost every night.

Daily walks in our neighborhood started with Jim riding in a backpack. As the girls came along this continued. It was exciting for me to see common, taken for granted things anew through their eyes. Frequent visits to nearby parks and beaches expanded our horizons. Garage sales became the source of many inexpensive and varied playthings. The favorite items related to daily living experiences. All three youngsters loved playing with their friends using their play kitchen set. Dolls and toy vehicles were also important to all three children. The conversations I overheard demonstrated the integral educational and play value these items contained.

Television introduced us to even more opportunities. We do carefully select the programs we watch. When Jim came home for his studies this was a struggle. He wanted to retreat from the world, and television would have allowed this escape. He has a tendency to become mesmerized by television and I had to limit his viewing of programs. At first he resisted and tried to sneak some extra viewing time, but this rebellion did not persist very long. Now I notice he has much more discrimination in his viewing habits.

Jim came home for his studies in March. Laurie was doing well at her school despite a change in principals that had created a severe morale problem among the teachers that affected the students and parents. She is very outgoing and easily makes the best of a poor situation, so she started fourth grade that fall. I did not personally know the teacher she was assigned to but was hopeful it would work out despite unsettling things I had heard about this teacher.

Five weeks later Dale and I went to Back To

School Night. As we left the classroom Dale was the one to speak first. He wanted Laurie at home. The teacher, who had taught for almost thirty years, firmly stated that no child in her classroom was going to be ahead of or behind any other child in the class. Every child was expected to work the very same math problem and read the very same page as every other child in the class. She appointed "Captains" who were to tell her everything that went on in the room when her back was turned because "children at that age like to tattle anyway."

No wonder Laurie had been complaining that her fingers hurt because of writing so much and that she hated being a "Captain." It turned out that because Laurie was ahead of most of the class the teacher made her do more math problems (simple subtraction in this case). Every other teacher she had had encouraged her to work to her own capacity. None had required her to monitor the actions of her fellow students.

I knew from the experience of friends there was no appeal to this principal. He had belittled other parents and made school life harder on their youngsters when the parents had tried to improve a bad classroom situation. That November I wrote to a friend, *"Home schooling is turning out to be so much easier on me than having Jim and Laurie in school. Time-wise, besides getting to be with them more, I find myself so much freer and not controlled by school activities. I did not notice it as much when they were all in the same elementary school but as they get older the demands on my time increased and were set by someone with no interest in family activities. And I am finding a side benefit in that I am brushing up on my own skills and learning new things. With the ages Jim and Laurie are they do most everything on their own. The only time I get myself hung up is whenever I start doubting myself and my own capability."*

Susan was going to another public school in the district, a modified Montessori program which suited her well. She flourished in an environment which allowed her more freedom to choose her activities and was stimulated by hands-on experiences. In kindergarten she participated in the IBM Writing to Read Lab. I was working in her classroom several times a week during kindergarten. In first grade she chose to write a "book" about the River Nile using high school books she picked up at the local school textbook depository. I was often in her classroom that year too.

But during first grade Susan started staying home "sick." When I talked to another mother in Susan's group I learned that her daughter was also refusing to go to school. We worked with the teacher who willingly worked with us to discover the cause. It turned out she had been ignoring her top group - since they were so capable - to spend more time with the four non-English speaking students and with youngsters in the slower group. Once she again started spending time with Susan's group things smoothed out somewhat (what are we *asking* of our teachers)?

But I still noticed the spark going out of Susan.

She started telling me that she needed more freedom to learn as she was ready and what she wanted to learn. She even wrote this down in a notebook. One day she told me, "School puts too much pressure on me. It makes me feel hot all over and uncomfortable. At school I can't learn what I want to when I want to."

Susan remained in the public school until the end of the first grade. But since then she has continued her studies at home and constantly expresses her appreciation. I am most grateful that she is able to tell me when something is not going well so we can adjust our own program to suit her present needs. Once when I was putting too much pressure on Susan to "produce" I found this note on my bedside stand next to the book I was reading: *"Dear Mom, I feel like I need a break (even if a short one) away. It's just I feel so cooped up here because I have to do a lot of stuff on schedule and have to do certain things. I don't have as much time to do stuff that I want to when I want to. I just feel so cooped up. When I was in public school I remember blinking back tears."*

When a television news reporter visited our home for an interview she emphatically told him that freedom to learn her own way best suits her educational needs. I resisted the temptation to coach the girls in any way in preparation for his interview. I realized I was taking a risk but I felt comfortable enough with my girls to allow this freedom of expression.

The reporter asked the girls how long they expect to home school. Laurie responded she would like to go to high school. Susan, on the other hand, stated she thinks she will wait until college. However this turns out will ultimately involve their own decisions as they do know what they want.

A few years ago I would have been horrified at the thought that a child can direct her own studies successfully. Now that I look around and see some of the poor choices adults make for children, and the ability children have to make intelligent choices if allowed to, I have reconsidered.

My children have been labeled as "gifted." This is a label I don't like when it connotes "my child is better than your child." I do not consider my children as better, only as individual children with their own talents, strengths, and weaknesses. This is a concept I have tried to impart constantly when speaking at or participating in parenting or education-related workshops and in private conversations.

I was delighted to receive a subscription renewal notice from *Gifted Children Monthly* written by James Alvino, Ph. D., publisher, which states, *"It used to be thought that giftedness is something a child was born with. Today we know otherwise. According to expert James J. Gallagher, 'We can create giftedness through designing enriched environments and opportunities, or we can destroy it by failing to create those environments and opportunities.'"*

My lifelong experiences have prepared me to implement the idea of interest initiated learning with my children. However, it is in retrospect that I discovered this fact. My background reading reinforced my thoughts as to what education is all about.

I came from a home where reading was important and went to a small one room school where I worked at my own pace and had plenty of tutors available. This laid the groundwork for me. I experienced teacher training that did not really teach me how to teach. This continued my education. I finally realized that "educational experts" do not have any more answers than I do as to how effective learning takes place. This forced me to the conclusion that I should truly start listening to my students. I now think that interest initiated learning is most effective when the learner has not already been "programmed in the system."

CHAPTER TWO

CHOOSING OUR LEARNING MATERIALS

A child can make better sense of the world on her own than we can do for her through adult produced curricula. My own children had to teach me the truth of this statement. I had been "schooled" to believe that certain trained adults are the only ones qualified to choose what is important to learn. Reluctantly I began to see the wisdom in listening to the student.

When we brought Jim home to do his schooling I did not believe I was capable of directing his studies. We enrolled him in a private school with independent study which could be done through the mail. I went to our school district textbook discard center to select what I considered appropriate books for Jim to study. I wanted to supplement the private school's textbooks on language arts, science, math, history, social studies, and music. Carefully I outlined a course of study for each subject. This contradicted my belief that I was incapable of directing his studies, although I did not realize this at the time.

Jim looked at what I had prepared without saying anything. He put the books in the box I gave him to file his school work. To please me he did some exercises I assigned in his U. S. History book. Eventually he stopped working on my assignments. His teacher's assignments fared a little better - but not much. I tried to work with him on some of the assignments I had given him. He did not want my help.

It was no wonder that he did not like the textbooks. I discovered by working with Jim how boring today's textbooks are. Publishers of textbooks claim that they are responding to the market, and to them this means that textbooks must present the subject in a manner that offends no one. They avoid the semblance of favoring one segment of our society over another. They claim they need to conform to current readability formulas.

His new correspondence teacher used better quality textbooks than I found. This encouraged me to search for more interesting materials. To my delight I uncovered many sources for outstanding materials. Now I was in a dilemma. There was so much available that I became overwhelmed by my choices. Jim was not delighted over my discoveries. Someone else's choices did not interest him.

I started to observe his interests. Reading the back issues of *Growing Without Schooling*, I found a few articles on older students leaving the school structure to begin home schooling. Parents, writing of their experiences, related that what their children needed most was time. They used the time to unwind, to heal, to dream, and to rediscover their interests. For some youngsters this required a year or more.

Sam, the son of my friend Laurie Struble, needed this time. I remember Laurie saying that it was a full year before he could handle learning activities as most people think of them. Sam started home schooling in the fourth grade. He chose to attend one year of public high school but then returned to home schooling. He passed the California High School Proficiency Test in April of 1988, and is now enrolled in classes at Allan Hancock College. When Laurie learned I was writing this book she wrote, *"Anyway, about how I got into home schooling... I had no idea such a thing was possible when Sam was little. I diligently searched for the best school situation for him. He did okay in kindergarten (at public school) but the social situation was bad. It was such a tender age to be forced into a situation like that. So for the first grade we tried private school. The kids were basically nicer there but it was SO strict, and pushed the kids academically. So it was back to the local public school for second grade. He did real well in school, but he didn't like it much and the social situation was still bad. So for the third grade we tried another school which was the first year as a public school 'back to basics' regime. It was terrible. That's when it all came to a head and we really started having problems. Sam was miserable. He'd wake up in the morning and say he wished he were sick so he wouldn't have to go to school. This bright, eager-to-learn little boy was totally burned out and tired of learning. The school system took his enthusiasm about learning away and 'busy worked' him into the ground. He was a natural born reader, but for a year after he left school he wouldn't look at a book. And to this day he hasn't overcome his aversion to math.*

"Thus started our experience with home schooling. And I became an immediate advocate. If ever a person were born to be 'unschooled' it was Sam. He did it all on his own. With his high linguistic intelligence, I never applied myself to 'teaching' him, I just supplied him with books. He's a voracious reader and will study a subject in depth all on his own. A wonderful example of interest initiated learning. And he learns most of the material thoroughly and retains it well, unlike most of what he was 'force fed' in school and quickly forgot."

Other than Laurie, I searched in vain for local families who were home schooling older students. I wrote letters to any possible source I could uncover, but everyone I found had only younger children, and I was not yet convinced that Laurie's interest initiated approach was at all effective.

That spring Dale and I attended a conference devoted to parenting topics that changed the way I regarded learning alternatives. I presented a session on school readiness with an emphasis on kindergarten, and the discussion period clarified my thoughts as I responded to questions from participants. After my session I attended a panel session that explored available learning alternatives. Panelists discussed the advantages of public and private schools, home schooling, and certain learning philosophies such as Waldorf and Montessori.

In the exhibit hall, at a booth for the Family Centered Learning Alternatives, we met Nancy Oh. I was beginning to suspect that Jim's independent study program was inappropriate for him, and Nancy showed us that it was possible to design a study program that considered the student's interests. Nancy and I became friends, and a month later she visited us while on her way to a home school conference. John Boston was sharing a ride with her to the conference, and I invited several friends to discuss home schooling with John and Nancy. That discussion became my turning point, as John changed my mind about the effectiveness of student interest initiated learning.

John Boston is the administrator of the School of Home Learning (now Home Centered Learning). His program operates on the principle of "invited teaching," which means the role of the teacher is to assist the student in locating and using the kinds of materials, services, and people she needs in order to learn what she wishes to know. John has secondary level teaching credentials and a master's degree. He noticed that unless his students had a personal reason for taking his class they were not retaining what he taught them. This bothered him. When he attempted to set up programs matching the interests of his students he faced opposition from fellow teachers and the administration.

Stella and John Boston brought their son, Sean, home to study when he was in the fifth grade because he was so miserable in school. I can still hear John chuckle as he recalled his first attempts to "teach" Sean at home. John decided Sean needed help with spelling so he set up elaborate lesson plans to accomplish this. *John's* spelling improved. Sean was not interested in learning to spell. However, when Sean decided for himself that he needed to spell correctly, he taught himself.

John is a firm believer in interest initiated learning. In his quiet way he encourages others to be open to its possibilities. He founded Home Centered Learning because of his belief in a minimum of adult interference in the learning process. After five years of experiencing interest initiated learning with Sean, John wrote an article for *Growing Without Schooling*. He reported the results of allowing Sean the freedom to learn in their home and their community. Sean developed high level social skills, and a psychologist tested him. He lacked certain memorization skills but his abilities were of college entrance level. Activities in which he was interested sharpened his reading and math skills. He loved to work on his Honda motorcycle which in turn led to an interest in automotive mechanics.

Sean received his high school diploma from the School of Home Learning in 1987 and is now attending college. In 1988 Palomar College awarded him the Don Erbe Automotive Scholarship, an award established to acknowledge and encourage college students in the automotive field. It requires demonstration of high interest through outside participation and accomplishments. Sean is also on the college's honor roll.

John and Nancy pointed out that I had already been practicing interest initiated learning with my children - and with great success. From the time they were babies, I had surrounded them with many learning opportunities. Jim had entered the Lucky Supermarket "21 Days of America" essay contest in June, 1984 and won a trip to Washington, D. C. for the family. His teacher had told me that more than what he learned in school, my parenting style had enabled him to win the contest. Other teachers made similar remarks, but I did not believe them. It was only after John and Nancy pointed out the same thing that I understood.

I looked back over Jim's 1985-86 school year. He was in the local middle school until March and received all A's on his report card despite his learning frustrations and all the time lost due to illness caused by stress. His favorite class was music, where he learned to play the bell lyre. He liked his teachers and his teachers liked him. But he was under so much stress that he was not able to effectively learn.

One assignment stands out in my memory. For English he had to write a descriptive paragraph. He chose to describe Sherlock Holmes' distinctive hat, but he became extremely frustrated because of time limitations. I often read aloud in the evenings and he loved the Sherlock Holmes stories, and he wanted to go into depth on the topic of Sherlock Holmes. But there was no time nor credit granted him for pursuing this topic.

He resented the assignments his independent study teacher gave him, as feedback took so long. He mailed his assignments to the teacher every two weeks, and she was prompt in answering, but the assignments were sometimes four weeks old before he received a response. He was not particularly interested in the assignments anyway. There was no pressure put on him to complete them, and his teacher recognized the need for a period of healing. She used this time for the two of them to get to know each other.

At first I felt that the time from March to June was rather bleak. Then I began to realize the valuable learning experiences that had occurred. Jim started working out in the yard. He became interested in growing things. By that summer he planted a small vegetable garden. He was pleased with the results. His garden was an ordinary one by some people's standards, but we thought it was outstanding.

Jim became interested in weather. We ordered a four way weather station that measured temperature, rainfall, wind direction, and wind speed. He faithfully recorded the rainfall. He and his grandfather, who lives two hundred miles north of us, compare our rainfall totals, and they often share weather observations. Weather conditions are important to my father because of his orchard, and so

Jim learned about fruit ranching also.

I subscribed to the magazine Gifted Children Monthly(no longer published). If Jim got to the mail before I did I had to wait to read it because he liked to read the "Spin Off" pages. Sometimes he even responded to some of their surveys and contests even though he has never enjoyed writing much. He did this on his own, without any coaching from me. The things I would encourage him to participate in usually did not appeal to him. Normally he did not read the rest of the articles in Gifted Children Monthly. However, I shared one article with him because of his interest in making money, and it was the beginning of his lasting interest in the stock market. The article, "Money Matters are 'Fun-ancials' for Children," was written by an attorney and financial writer whose special interest is investor education. She encourages teaching children how to invest their money, and her article shows how to invest $1,000 and then follow your investment, making changes as you go along to increase your investment. Jim read the article thoroughly and for almost two years formed his own portfolio, following its progress and reading the stock market section of our newspaper.

While he no longer keeps records on how his "portfolio" is doing, he still follows the ups and downs of the stock market. He loves to discuss the stock market with his grandfather, and they get into some interesting discussions on investing money. To this day Jim reads The Wall Street Journal when he visits his grandfather, and his dream is to set aside enough money to invest on his own.

One advertisement in *Gifted Children Monthly* caught Jim's attention. *The Almaniac: The World Trivia Contest* is a challenge not of what you know, but of what you can find out. The competition is stiff and the questions can be tricky, but all the answers are contained in the current <u>World Almanac and Book of Facts</u>. Four contests are featured each year, with two taken directly from the <u>World Almanac</u>, one using Rand McNalley world maps (for their *Circumglobal Trophy Dash*), and one using North American maps. Jim loved the intense research needed to complete the contests.

The contests covered a wide range of topics. Under sports one question asked: *In which state is the football stadium of the greatest capacity? a) California, b) Michigan, c) Pennsylvania.* The answer booklet was quite specific: California's Rose Bowl was the largest. If someone said Michigan they were quickly reminded that Michigan has the largest college stadium but the question was not limited to colleges. Careful research was necessary to answer their sometimes tricky questions. But the answer booklets even specify exact pages certain answers can be found on. For instance, in the same contest with the above sports question was one on religion: *In terms of percentage of population, what is the most religious part of the world? a) Africa, b) Asia, c) Oceania, d) South America.* The answer according to the 1986 <u>World Almanac</u> was Oceania. It's 79% beats South America's 76%. The answer could be found on page 336 under Religion - Population, world.

Other topics in the 1986 contest included the

Arctic, facts about the United States, the Presidency, science, astrophysics, and even a few questions on Individual Retirement Accounts. The map contests are even more of a challenge. For the fun of it I worked on one that featured actual railroad maps in a portion of China and learned fascinating facts about the geography of China.

The answer sheet is sent out promptly after the close of the contest. Each participant is given a final summary booklet and participants may challenge a given answer, with credit given for challenged answers and credit statistics about the participants. About 1,000 people participate each time, with the average age being in the mid-thirties, and very few participants under 20. Jim usually placed somewhere in the middle, though where he placed did not concern him. He just enjoyed the challenge, but because the contests are time consuming he has not entered since starting to high school.

Jim did not want any assistance with any of the contests so I generally contented myself with browsing through them after he had sent his entries in. I was very impressed with the quality of these contests. Jim received a broad range of information through them and his research skills were definitely heightened.

Jim has a talent for mathematics. Susan does too. Dale, being an engineer, is strong in math skills. Laurie and I are more talented in writing skills than math. We enrolled Jim in the Young Scholar's Program at the University of California at Santa Barbara. UCSB College of Creative Studies created this program for middle school and high school students with aptitude in math, literature, science, and art. This program worked well for Jim and he was assigned a tutor for algebra.

Because the commute to the UCSB campus was difficult for us Jim only participated for one quarter. Through a friend we located a local high school senior who came to our house twice a week. At first the young man was not certain he could tutor, but it did not take long for Jim and Mayur to develop a good working relationship. Mayur's father has a Ph. D. in mathematics, and he told Mayur that algebra was the keystone to all higher math. At first Mayur could not understand what his father meant, but one day he said to me, "At last 1 know what my father means. Now algebra makes sense to me. I see how it works with higher mathematics because of working with Jim."

Jim had 12 hours of instruction in algebra at UCSB and approximately another 30 hours at home. Yet he covered more than a year's worth of algebra according to the high school counselor. He went directly into geometry in high school although our district requires incoming freshmen to take algebra. He also qualified to take advanced computer programming classes on the strength of his algebra experience.

Another math experience our youngsters have is keeping records for their newspaper routes. Upon acquiring their routes, both Jim and Laurie set up bookkeeping records that they are expected to maintain. Now that income tax laws have changed, even paper carriers need to file income tax and pay social security. When we set up their bookkeeping we did not realize how advantageous this was to become. Both of them now know their way around income tax forms because they are considered self-employed by the IRS. Dale has prepared our taxes for years and taken tax courses so he was able to help Jim and Laurie with theirs.

We have lively discussions concerning history, geography, and differing cultures throughout the world. We spent a whole year studying various holiday traditions throughout the world. Susan added her own information from a used text book she acquired from discarded library books. I had outline maps that we marked up according to the countries involved. This turned out to be a painless, fun way to learn geography. Susan again added her own twist as she loved the maps which had mileage scales.

Spelling improved with each child the more they read. We all enjoy some variety of word puzzles, and this too has helped our spelling. The youngsters prefer the word puzzle books from the supermarket magazine racks such as Penny Press and Dell. Jim's particular favorite type of puzzles are the Logic ones. Susan especially enjoys doing the cryptograms. All three enjoy crossword and word search puzzles, but I quickly noticed that they did not enjoy word puzzles intended for children as much because they were too simple and uninteresting.

I did attempt formal spelling lessons but the

three of them quickly let me know they did not consider the spelling lessons a learning experience.
When their uncle visited us and wanted to send
postcards to friends he asked the girls to help him
with many words as he is a notoriously poor speller.
I could not help wondering where they had learned
to spell so well since I had not taught them, but
even the difficult words he asked of them came easy
to the girls.

Pat, another home schooling friend, told me
one day of an experience she had with her eight year
old Melissa. At that time Pat was following the Cal-
vert lessons, and one of the spelling words was "apple." On every spelling test Melissa had no trouble
spelling apple. One day Pat was getting ready to do
her grocery shopping and she asked Melissa to add
apples to the shopping list. At the store she noticed
Melissa had misspelled "apple." When Pat asked
her why she never misspelled it on her tests, yet had
misspelled it on the list, Melissa told her that she
had only learned to get it right on the tests. Once Pat
let up on spelling tests she noticed a great improvement in Melissa's spelling.

California Education Code Section 51210 and
51220 list the required branches of study. The Education Code is specific only in certain areas, in these
areas only broad categories of reasonable knowledge
are specified. Grades one through six requirements
include: English, mathematics, science, fine arts, and
fire prevention. Social science, health, public safety
and accident prevention, and environmental issues
are more specific.

Social science is to include 1) the early history of California, 2) a study of the role and contributions of both men and women, black Americans, American Indians, Mexican, Asians, Pacific Island people, and other ethnic groups, to the economic, political, and social development of the United States, with particular emphasis on portraying the roles of these groups in contemporary society, and 3) a foundation for understanding the wise use of natural resources.

Health needs to include the effects of alcohol, narcotics, drugs and tobacco upon the human body, and physical education. Public safety and accident prevention courses are to include emergency first aid instruction, instruction in hemorrhage control, treatment for poisoning, resuscitation techniques, and cardio-pulmonary resuscitation when appropriate equipment is necessary. Environmental issues to be covered are the protection and conservation of resources, including the necessity for the protection of our environment.

Because my youngsters love to read I find that I have no trouble whatever meeting the state requirements as to subjects to be taught. My primary function is to oversee that the requirements are met. Our community surrounds us with opportunities to meet the state requirements. Field trips our home school support group plans give us a social setting in which to meet many of these requirements.

Our town gives us many opportunities to study early California history first hand. We have one of the missions that form the California mission chain, and its restoration is nearly complete. The mission's docent program puts us in the spirit of mission days. La Purissima mission was chosen as one of only six historic areas in California for our state's celebration of the U. S. Constitution bicentennial in the joint state and Post Cereals "Pop into the Past" celebration. We enjoyed special activities that day. The girls dressed up in authentic Chumash Indian attire of the mission days for the event. The docents present many historical reenactments throughout the year at the mission.

Local Chumash Indians present aspects of early California Indian life. Laurie attended a four hour session sponsored by the local museum on Indian skills and crafts. She made thread, prepared food, formed an arrowhead, and learned to start a fire using twigs during the day's activities. Periodically the local Parks and Recreation Department sponsors walking history tours which we have attended. This is a field trip we especially enjoy as the tour guide is so interesting and likeable.

We cover health and public safety issues by reading and discussion. Again there are many community resources available to us. We go on field trips to our fire station, water treatment plant, police station, and medical facilities. The Red Cross offers high quality first aid and babysitting courses of which we take advantage. The California State Department of Education requires AIDS instruction. I prepared a course on the subject only to discover all three youngsters were already well and accurately informed on the subject because of their observation and listening skills.

We often have informal spontaneous discussions. The youngsters present me with a synopsis of what they have absorbed. What an example they give me of the truth of what happens when you trust students to learn what is important. They show me my role as teacher is to guide and provide the resources.

Sometimes I will introduce a topic only to find that they are not interested, and nothing will make them learn if they do not find a subject interesting. I get immediate feedback that is unmistakable. In a formal school setting the demands on the teacher's time and attention made it impossible for them to freely express their lack of interest.

I fight a losing battle when I try to force my children to learn something that has no immediacy or meaning to their lives. I am still having to struggle with this, as the "teacher" and "mother" in me says that I know what is best for them. Yet every time I allow them to choose their own course of learning I am amazed at how well they have chosen for themselves. I do not necessarily know what or how my children should learn something unless I make the time and effort to listen to what they are saying by word and action.

In 1985 the State of California published the *Model Curriculum Standards: Grades Nine Through Twelve*. The emphasis is on reading skills because they foresee that more than half of the job openings in the future will require people with high-level skills in reading, comprehension, and thinking. With the schools' preoccupation on basic skills, researchers and teachers have noticed that while students have learned basic language arts and computational skills, they do not have a sense of how to use those skills to advantage in their lives.

Model Curriculum Standards acknowledges that these reading, comprehension, and thinking skills require cooperation. Home environment is the most influential element, and they even state that home is the first school. Those children who have homes where reading is enjoyed, literacy is valued, and interest in academic achievement is shown are the students who have a head start in educational institutions. After home, libraries are listed in the report as crucial to learning. Only *then* do the writers of this curriculum guide list educational institutions.

The teacher-student relationship is vital to the educational experience. The active and responsible agents in education must be the students. The authors state that nothing worth learning can be taught: "Students must themselves come to grips with major texts and with the difficult tasks of thinking and composing and articulating ideas into language."

Jim is searching for a job that will pay him more than his paper route does. He learned of the page position at our local public library so filled out the application form. During the process he realized how much experience he had accumulated and how many people were glad to serve as references for him. Besides his paper route he had tutored other children in our home school support group. The mothers could not praise him enough and the children he worked with still think he is the greatest friend they could have.

He went for his interview. After a half hour of talking with him, the library director and her assistant took him to a cart loaded with books patrons had returned. They told him to sort the books into categories. Jim's remark when he came home was, "That part was easy because it was just like sorting my baseball cards." He has thousands of baseball cards sorted into many boxes and knows exactly where each one is and its value. Until this happened my husband had been skeptical of any redeeming value to Jim's card collection.

Somehow we adults have to trust our children's choices of learning experiences. At times Jim has resisted my attempts to guide his studies. When I let him lead the way in curriculum choices, I notice he often surprises me and delights me with the results. His choices are usually better than mine because he knows himself far better than I do.

Chapter Three

Scheduling Our Learning Opportunities

Nine year old Susan just announced to me that she is thinking of a funny poem. While I am writing this she is engrossed in her composition. From experience I know that what she is producing is far better than any assignment that I could give her. Her pattern of literary accomplishments includes periods of barrenness followed by imaginatively written creations. Her imagination is vivid and lively, but she hates to be prodded into writing. Of the three youngsters she is the most adamant about not doing something she does not want to do.

At home she has the freedom to write creatively when she is ready no matter what day or time of day it is. Nothing squashes her writing faster than telling her that she *has* to write something right now. No threats are severe enough to make her write something if she does not want to.

It is Friday. Susan has finished her poem and is singing to herself as she makes patterns with her Hama beads. She is delighted that I asked her permission to share her poem with you:

The Boring Day
Today is Saturday
It is such a boring day
I have no school, no written rule
I have no friends to talk to when class ends
I have no letters to write and also nothing to sight
I have no cards to sign and no letters to align
I have no calendars, books, letters, pledges to read because
I've just been freed
I have no friends to play with
I have no books/scripts to read because
I've just been freed
Today is such a boring day
I wish it would never end.

Observing my three youngsters closely has impressed upon me two important aspects of effective, long lasting learning. I notice these same traits in myself, and I've discovered several books and articles which also cite these two principles of learning.

First: there are individual learning rhythms of advance and retreat and of exploration and consolidation of ideas which often cannot be predicted or controlled. Second: students need both time and opportunity to reflect on the barrage of information to which they are exposed.

Are we sending wrong information to our children when we insist that only activities performed at certain times of the day or on certain days of the week count as "learning?" In a nationally televised interview in August, 1988, a National Education Association official declared that only learning which takes place during designated hours of the day compatible with state programs is valid.

In September, 1988, a local television station sent a reporter to our house for an interview on home schooling. I did not coach the girls beforehand, but they proved to me that all our students need is our trust in them. The reporter stayed an hour and a half, taping most of that time. In the small portion of the interview which was televised that night on the news, both girls clearly expressed that they thought the greatest advantage they have in their present learning experience is the freedom to study what they want when they want. Both girls declared that that is the way they learn best.

One day I was chatting with a teacher who has a combination fourth, fifth, sixth grade class by choice. She is well known in the district as a superb teacher. She told me she wished she could either work with her own boys at home or find a program similar to what I do with my children. Then she related how the previous weekend the family camped at a local lake. Her youngest son spent about five hours with an elderly fisherman discussing fish and the art of fishing. Her closing statement was that those few hours were more valuable to her son than the previous month of school work had been, yet that experience would never show up on any school records.

My youngsters have their own individual learning rhythms. At first I worried about whether I was harming them by allowing them periods of reflection. I noticed that there could be long periods of time in which nothing seemed to be accomplished. These times of daydreaming and quiet reflection last for a few hours or even for a couple of weeks. Mostly they last for only a few days. Just when I start getting concerned the youngsters will astound me with the gigantic leaps in learning that have taken place during - and because of being allowed to have - their quiet periods.

During this time they usually strongly resist my efforts to impose any new materials or instruction I may have to offer. Instead they prefer to sit outside or in their rooms just staring off into space. Sometimes they will express boredom, but not too often. On the surface they do not seem to be doing much reading while in the phase, yet when I observe unobtrusively, I do notice that their choices tend to be more in depth reading than light reading.

Laurie struggles more than Jim or Susan with math concepts. However, once she grasps them, they stay with her. Multiplication of multiple digits was particularly difficult for her. No matter how many examples Dale or I used, she could not understand why you have to offset by one digit when you perform the addition operation in multiplication of multiple digits. We set aside math and went on to other topics. In the meantime she went into a reflective mood. We were preparing for a trip to visit grandparents in Minnesota so I figured there would be plenty of time to get back to math later on. Our first night on the trip we were eating supper at our motel restaurant when Laurie started doodling on her paper napkin. Her face lit up as she proudly proclaimed, "I got it!" She showed us her napkin filled with multiplication of multiple digits accurately done. There had been no outward indication that she had even been thinking of math all those intervening weeks.

Susan usually spends days at a time in her reflective moods sitting out in our backyard. We have a particularly interesting yard as it is tiered in three levels and each level is different. There are marvelous fruit trees to climb and birds and other interesting creatures are attracted by our four fish ponds.

Susan will sit for hours observing the teeming life out there. She was the first one to notice that we had baby goldfish swimming among the hundreds of tadpoles. Never before had baby goldfish survived so at first we did not believe her. We had to admit that she did indeed know what she was talking about when she told us she had seen the goldfish mate and lay their eggs even though no one else had.

One evening eight year old Susan and I were watching the evening news. She turned and solemnly told me, "I like to make up my own mind about issues. That is why I read so much and listen to the news, so I can decide for myself what is true." From there she launched into a deep discussion about the Greenhouse Effect, a subject I had no idea she knew about. Her discussion demonstrated a deep understanding of the issues involved.

Susan often writes me notes. She gave me these unsolicited writings after going through some periods of daydreaming. Both were written at the age of eight: *"The light needs electricity from the battery from both sides so you have to touch the right ones together to turn on the light. You need bare wire so the electricity can get on the wire to go inside the light tube."* After her note she demonstrated her observation using a battery, wire, and a flashlight bulb.

"My explanation of how dinosaurs died. The plants started dying and became scarce, so since there wasn't any food, the plant eaters started to die. Soon the meat eaters discovered that and started eating each other. Soon there was only one left and with no food to eat it died too. What happened to the plants was it got too cold in some parts of the earth and too hot in others, and the land had started to shift."

In elementary school Jim developed an intense dislike for anything labeled science. On our trip to Minnesota we stopped at the Grand Canyon for two days. He was fascinated by his surroundings but did not say much. Then we went on one of the ranger-led geology walks. Since it was late in May Jim, Laurie and Susan were the only youngsters on the walk of about fifty participants. The ranger asked several geology related questions. Jim, who is usually very quiet and not given to answer questions, raised his hand for every one of them and astounded Dale and I by answering each one confidently. We had seen no evidence of his choosing to study geology, yet even the ranger was impressed with his knowledge.

While our days do have a certain amount of structure to them, nothing is rigidly adhered to if something more interesting occurs. The youngsters get up at seven, fix their own breakfasts, do their chores, and then start the day's academic activities by eight. From eight to noon we concentrate on these academic activities according to each person's needs. The afternoon usually finds a continuation of the morning's activities as well as doing paper routes and outside activities such as Campfire meetings. We have an early supper followed by a quiet evening. Friends come and go throughout the afternoon and evening. Bedtime is around nine. Normally, each one reads for awhile before falling asleep.

In keeping with my philosophy that learning is not confined by time of year, week, or day, I choose to "school" year round. If some event which we consider valuable occurs on weekends, evenings, or holidays, it counts for their learning accomplishments.

We have an excellent theatrical group connected with a local community college that puts on outdoor performances on summer evenings. Susan developed an interest in Shakespeare all on her own at the age of seven when she pulled my copy of The

Complete Works of Shakespeare from the bookcase. When she was nine the PCPA Theater Group announced their presentation of *The Tempest*. Susan and I read the play aloud in preparation. She could hardly contain herself because of her delight as the play unfolded before her eyes that night. In fact she recognized one of the characters before I did when he came on stage. Laurie saw no necessity to reading the play before we attended the performance. I have no doubt that the next time PCPA puts on a Shakespearean play, she will be the first to read the play.

One of Laurie's greatest pleasures is to put on a play, whether it is one she has made up or not. In 1986 we attended a conference for homeschoolers. A wonderful gentleman offered to work with the youngsters while the parents attended the sessions. Herb Hammer led them in producing short skits and plays, some were spontaneous and others were prepared. At the end of the day the children displayed their talents to the attendees. This was Laurie's introduction to the joys of putting on plays, and theater got into Laurie's blood.

We attended a four day National Coalition of Alternative Community Schools conference in Escondido, California. Once again Herb led youngsters in putting on small plays for the four hundred participants in the conference. This cemented a very special relationship between Herb and our children, especially Laurie, and since then Herb has encouraged Laurie's interest in theater. He travels two hundred miles to attend performances that Laurie produces for our local home schooling families.

One day Laurie saw a notice that the local Civic Theater group was auditioning for *The Best Christmas Pageant Ever*. The book, by Barbara K. Robinson, is one of our favorite stories. Both Laurie and Susan auditioned and were given parts. Laurie had a small speaking part but also was understudy for one of the major parts as the director was taking no chances of illness closing the play down. From October through the ninth and final performance in mid December, we were at the theater around twenty hours a week.

We focused our learning experience around the play. After the close of the play one mother told me that her daughter's grades at school had suffered because of her involvement in the play. So often the truly valuable learning experiences do not count because they do not take place during "school hours."

A home schooling family with four boys, living on an island in the province of Ontario, Canada, spent the night with us while traveling through California. We compared our experiences and found that each year our approach to learning varies according to the needs expressed by the children. Mikell said that her first year was structured, but loosely. As she and the boys became more confident all structure to their days and activities was removed. They are in their fourth year and each year has been different. Now the boys are asking for some structure again.

These boys love life and love learning. It was inspiring to be around them. They could as easily discuss ocean life (something they had never seen before) as they could computers. They were fascinated with the history of California as it fit in with what they had been seeing on this trip. They could figure out mileage already covered and related costs despite not having had formal math classes.

Since California requires 180 days of school, I use a year round configuration. This means nine weeks of class and four weeks of break in record keeping each quarter. Just as many learning activities occur during the four week break as during the time of the nine week quarters. The main difference is that I am not keeping as detailed records of these experiences.

Even on days when they are sick, they continue learning according to the energy available. While they were in school, I noticed that sick days were "do nothing" days. Now sick days are quiet activity days in which learning continues.

Each quarter I single out two or three major areas we will concentrate on. In this way I am assured that we are covering all the state requirements. At the same time I am exposing the youngsters to topics they might not otherwise have chosen or known about. Sometimes these topics are not enthusiastically received, but that is all right with me as I know that at least I have introduced them, and it is up to the youngsters to explore further if and when they choose.

One quarter we went into detail on the human body using the Invisible Man and Invisible Woman models, district textbooks, Dover anatomy books, and various newspaper and magazine articles. Each youngster reacted differently as I presented the material. That same quarter we worked on typing skills. This they found boring but I insisted that they work on it at least for the quarter as I consider typing skills important. Our third area of concentration was organizing a state wide home school day with day long meetings and workshops. The children each contributed to the success of that day. Those were our areas of concentration for that quarter, but reading, communication, and computational skills were not neglected.

Another quarter we used the TOPS science unit on magnetism while at another time we used the same science series on pendulums. Both of these units were popular, and the youngsters enjoyed all the hands on activities provided. Susan went on from the magnetism unit to an interest in electronics, so we bought the Radio Shack Electronic Project Kit with 160 activities for her. She goes in spurts of interest. It will sit on the shelf for months, then she will use it extensively, writing up the results of her experiments in the book provided.

In our study of the contributions many different cultures have made to our American way of life, we devoted a quarter to using the Good Apple Activity Book entitled *Americans, Too!* This challenging book promotes understanding of American minorities through research related activities. Since the girls avidly read the newspaper, I find that we get into some stimulating discussions on related topics.

During 1987 we devoted three quarters to studying American History and the U.S. Constitution as part of the Constitutional Bicentennial celebration. Because Jim had won the trip to Washington, D.C. in 1985, we could build on what we had seen during that trip. Since the youngsters were personally involved, they were much more interested. All three participated in essay and poster contests about the Constitution that year. Susan won an award from *Gifted Children Monthly* for her poster.

The book that Susan won for her poster is Kids' America by Steven Caney. This book is now a family favorite, and a source of many hours of activities. Susan constantly refers to it. Among other things it contains articles on magic, weather forecasting, sign language, genealogy, frog jumping, and many more adventures. Along with activities you find beloved tales and legends.

During a contest sponsored by our public library, Laurie won several books for drawing a poster on the value of reading (within two days she had read the books). Her age group had the largest number of contributions so she was particularly pleased with herself.

My youngsters do not like using workbooks. All three youngsters have said that when in school they primarily wanted to get done with the workbook pages and did not really learn the topic at hand. They said that many times classmates would just hurry through the pages not caring about correct answers. I had corrected workbook pages for Laurie's second grade teacher and had noticed that myself. Sometimes, Laurie told me, she did her work correctly but still did not understand why she was doing it. In one of her classes workbooks were used both as a form of busywork and as punishment.

Susan did not have excessive workbook experience in school. But her Sunday school teacher started assigning workbook pages as homework. To the teacher's consternation parents came to her asking her not to do this as their youngsters were being swamped with workbook activities at school. I had noticed Susan balking at her assignments even though she loves her Sunday school teacher. Susan complained that she did not like doing these workbook pages. As soon as the teacher let up on workbook pages Susan and her class settled down happily.

When I find an especially attractive and well done workbook I will try it. We are selective in which pages and which activities we do in the workbook and I am careful to give immediate feedback on pages done. I do have several workbooks just lying around which I thought were great, but the youngsters vigorously disagreed with me. When they themselves choose one, however, I notice that the workbook is almost always well used.

I find it interesting that in one of the supplementary materials catalogs the publisher felt it necessary to devote nine pages to justifying the value of workbooks. There is no substitute to judicial use of workbooks. Used creatively, workbooks can motivate youngsters. Research shows and people experienced with working with children know that you learn to read by reading and to write by writing, not by filling in blanks.

When I use workbooks I have found that they are most effective if you keep several things in mind. Use workbooks that reinforce concepts which you have already introduced. Be certain that students understand what they are to do. Select appropriate workbook pages related to your topic and matched to the student's abilities. Periodically discuss with students how they arrived at their answers. They can surprise you with their depth of thinking! This also gives you an opportunity to discover any misunderstanding of the material. Provide opportunity for cooperative learning with their peers. Use the workbook as a chance to develop related topics or activities.

When our family becomes engrossed with a particular project we continue with it unless something else demands our immediate attention. Our schedule has to be quite flexible in order to allow for this. Sometimes we work on an joint project, but more often projects are individual.

I do not find working with three different ages at the same time has presented much difficulty. On their cooperative days, they help each other with projects or when one is having difficulty understanding something. On their uncooperative days, nothing would help anyway. They are constantly having to adjust their own needs to the needs of someone else, and this of itself is an invaluable lesson on life. The more refined their basic skills become, the more independently they learn. All I need to do is stand aside and be ready to provide necessary resources.

Television plays its part in our learning. There are some worthwhile programs. We do limit the amount of time that television is on and many days we do not use it at all. We all like watching three excellent programs on public television. *Square One* clarifies math concepts. Laurie had no problem understanding prime numbers after watching their presentation. For science we watch *Newton's Apple* and *3-2-1 Contact.*

Another fascinating science program, *Mr. Wizard's World*, is only on cable television. Some of the educational programs produced for the school system on public television have been very useful to us. Jim learned useful art techniques from some of the programs on how to draw. Susan likes to watch the wild animal programs on public television and on cable television's Discovery Channel.

It is an advantage to have a VCR. Often we tape a program to watch at a more convenient time. One winter *In The Attic*, Meip's story of how she hid Anne Frank and her family during World War II, was on late in the evening. We taped it and watched it at an appropriate time as we were studying the effects of war. With a look of disbelief and tears close to falling, Laurie asked me, "Mom, is this a true story? Did people really treat other people like that?"

During the October, 1987 Los Angeles earthquake, we stayed by our television listening to seismologists explain earthquakes and viewing the damage an earthquake can cause. California schools are required to give instruction in earthquake safety. My girls had been given the proper instruction each year, but nothing is more impressive than to have the event occur close to home (we did not feel it) and to see the aftermath graphically presented. We all learned new facts that morning. Laurie was so fascinated that she ordered more earthquake materials to study.

We followed the Presidential primaries, campaign, and election closely using television, newspapers, and a marvelous poster from *Weekly Reader* on which we recorded the results of each primary. As each candidate dropped out of the race, he was crossed off our chart. Even Susan was interested in following the progress of the campaign.

Games are a rich source of learning materials. Part of our interest in the Presidential election was heightened by playing *Hail to the Chief*, produced by Aristoplay. The faces and some facts about each of our Presidents are easier to remember because we play this game. When we play no one loses points for not knowing the answer as long as he or she repea. ' e answer back. That way mom is not embarrassed because she forgot (or worse yet, did not know) the answer, and the youngsters do not feel bad because they don't know the answer. Since the Presidents are in sequence on the playing board it is simple to get a cohesive feeling for our country's rich history. The map of the states with their capitals which you travel on the campaign trail impresses you with the vastness of the west and the denseness of the population on the east coast.

We have found that the games produced by Aristoplay are of exceptional quality and value. *Hail to the Chief* was the first one I bought. Since then we have purchased several more and I have not been disappointed in any of them. *Made for Trade* acquaints you with early American colonial life as you barter and trade on your journey through town. *Where in the World?* was an instant success with the family as we learn world geography painlessly. You are able to play this game in many different ways by focusing on populations, capitals, major religions, languages, exports, imports, or monetary units. *By Jove* pits us mortals against the Roman and Greek Gods as we try to snatch the Golden Fleece and maneuver the Labyrinth. *Music Maestro* introduced us to old as well as modern musical instruments, and *Art Deck* increases our awareness of master painters.

We even found a game that teaches nutrition. *Super Sandwich*, produced by Teaching Concepts, Inc., is based on planning well balanced dietary habits. You must purchase foods that meet your recommended Dietary Allowance of protein, calcium, iron, Vitamin A, Vitamin B-complex and Vitamin C and yet not exceed the calorie allowance. Trips to the "gym" are often necessary during the game. The girls enjoy this game, and I have noticed that their knowledge of nutrition has changed as a result of playing it.

An old favorite game of mine from childhood was *Authors*. I was not certain how the youngsters would react, but could not resist purchasing it too. It is our most frequently played game. They especially love to ask for a book we have read and they look for opportunities to read those with which they are not familiar. As a child I had to memorize *The Charge of the Light Brigade* by Tennyson. Because this game is listed on the *Authors* cards, we read it. Susan now goes around the house reciting it for the sheer joy of hearing the words roll off her tongue.

Games play an important part in our learning experiences. We aim to keep competition at a minimum most of the time. This has worked well as no one is hesitant to play because they might not know the answers. At times something comes up in a game that stimulates exploration of the subject in greater depth.

Games of strategy also have their place in our education. Susan and I often play *Craze*, a challenging math game that includes an element of luck to make it more interesting. You use any possible math operation with the numbers shown on the three dice you have tossed, with the object of being the first to cross off a given square on the grid. There is a rather complex method of computing your score, but Susan quickly mastered that part.

There are so many games from which to choose. I generally make my choices after reading about the games in a review or a catalog which provides greater description. Recommendation from people whose opinion I trust is another determinant. There are some companies that you know from experience provide quality items. The *Presents For The Promising* catalog from *Gifted Children Magazine* is a good source of information about games (second edition update: *Gifted*

Children Magazine is no longer published, and the *Presents for the Promising* catalog is no longer available). A local educational toy store has also been an invaluable resource for me as they will let me look at the game before purchase.

We use these games as an integral part of our flexible schedule. Learning takes place during these games. Sometimes there is a noticeable awareness of learning occurring right before my eyes. Most of the time, however, I discover much later how much knowledge they gained in the process of playing a certain game. Why can't learning be fun as well as work?

Marco Meirovitz, author, educator, and inventor of the game *Mastermind*, wrote an article in *Gifted Children Monthly* titled, "What's in a Game?" He says few people realize the full potential of games to develop and strengthen thinking skills. He claims that games prepare us to face school, home, and work situations more easily. According to him, perceptive educators realize that education must provide students with tools for effective thinking, not just more knowledge. Games are the simplest and most pleasurable ways to accomplish this.

Skills learning in game playing include problem solving, creative thinking, memory, visualization, and communication. Other benefits to game playing are coordinating body movements with thinking (psychomotic activity), planning (strategy), discovering rules (inductive logic), and using information (deductive logic).

Game playing is a practical tool for improving thinking skills because students *want* to play and therefore will willingly practice. This practice does not become boring because each time the game is played it is different. Having fun provides motivation for learning.

Games reflect life because all the basic skills can be used such as memory, strategy, logic, creativity, communication, and problem solving, and these thinking skills are utilized in a responsive, dynamic environment. Games build self-confidence as they can be played at different levels according to the participants' abilities. The social process (learning to communicate, cooperate, compete in real life situations) promotes the use of imagination and trying out of new roles. It is possible to develop personality and expand life experiences through games.

When I was reading Meirovitz' article, I thought immediately of Laurie's favorite game, *Clue.* He compares a doctor diagnosing a patient's illness to the process required in many games. The doctor has to eliminate possibilities by testing (asking questions), getting more information, eliminating groups of illnesses, and proceeding through other tests until he determines the illness. The doctor with the best way of grouping possibilities and eliminating them finds the fastest solution. He adds that the same is true for many other professions: car mechanics, appliance repairmen, scientists, chemists, etc. Each must obtain information and find an effective way to keep track of that information. Games provide practice in these skills.

Jim learned to play the bell lyre while in middle school. He had never played a musical instrument before. This class proved to be the one class in middle school that he enjoyed. Between September and the following February he learned the basics of reading music. The girls taught themselves to read music (my own music background is sparse so I could not assist them). We have an electronic keyboard, some recorders, the bell lyre, and a xylophone which they use.

Most of our art activities center on crafts. Susan is teaching herself the art of rug braiding and is learning how to use the sewing machine as a result. Laurie taught herself how to knit and crochet and has recently taken up counted cross-stitch. And we all do needlepoint, including Jim.

An excellent resource for many different art activities which we use is *KidsArt News*. Kim Solga's publication is a bargain that can't be beat. She introduces readers to a wide range of art activities and appreciation, including the fine arts. Her explanations on how to do a project are clear and concise. Susan constantly refers to back issues for ideas when she is ready for a new activity.

Learning is a highly individual matter. It is important to provide the opportunities for learning to occur and be nurtured. With our flexible schedule we strive to enhance learning experiences according to the individual needs of each of our children. When I "schedule" learning activities spontaneity suffers.

There is so much information available today that was not available twenty years ago. What was taught in science and technology in the fifties is now obsolete, and this period of time has been labelled as the age of the information explosion. With diligent searching I do locate some workbooks that keep us up to date on information. But I find it necessary to use them only when my youngsters regard them as useful.

We prefer to teach our children how to research answers in order to have the latest information. And then we show them how to be able to continually update that information. We prefer to teach them to think for themselves rather than parrot back information that someone else deems important. By allowing Jim, Laurie, and Susan time to reflect on this barrage of information to which they are exposed, I believe their education will have a firm foundation on which to build throughout their lives.

Our youngsters have demonstrated to us that there are learning rhythms of advance in knowledge and then retreat to quietly consider the knowledge gained. This consolidation of assimilated knowledge cannot be predicted or controlled. Every time I have interfered with this rhythm I have broken a fragile phase in their learning. It is not always easy for me to step back to allow the periods of quiet reflection to do their work.

Workbooks sometimes give me a false sense of security until I receive feedback from my youngsters as to a particular workbook's value to them. I can offer information but I cannot force my children to be receptive to that information. People are uncomfortable when they are in a situation where they feel they have no control at all. Being uncomfortable is not conducive to learning. Just because I am an adult does not mean I know what is best for Jim, Laurie, and Susan.

Students rebel, even though they may not show it outwardly, when they do not feel control over a learning situation. This is why I offer my children learning opportunities and then try something else when I meet with resistance in them. As soon as I hear groans from them when I bring out a particular workbook I know without a shadow of a doubt that use of that workbook will produce questionable results. If the written work is sloppily done results are unmistakable. The work was done only because I said they HAD to do it. Add a few tears and I'm really in trouble!

We have had success with a few workbooks. In most cases one of the youngsters chose it. Very few times has one I have chosen been received enthusiastically. I am convinced that the success of a workbook depends on the interest of the student. Telling them to do it because "it is for your own good" just does not work in my family. And I am glad of it!

CHAPTER FOUR

TRUSTING
OUR CHILDREN
TO LEAD THE WAY

Susan often picks up a book to read on a subject in which I have had no clue she has any interest. At the age of seven she chose some high school books on electricity. An experiment in one of the books caught her eye. Following the directions, and with her father's assistance in locating the proper materials, she constructed her own question/answer board that lights up a bulb when you pick the correct answer (a low cost version of *Questron*). She amazed us with what doing that one project taught her. The next morning she proceeded to tell me why our family room light would come on when we flipped the switch. We had never discussed this, she just figured it out from what happened in her project.

Trusting our children to lead the way depends

greatly upon recognition of two basic principles. The first one is that the amount a person can learn at a given moment depends on how she feels about her ability to do the work. The second one is that interest initiated learning allows the student to utilize her abilities in the optimal manner. The old saying, "You can lead a horse to water, but you can't make him drink," expresses the futility of forcing a student to learn something when she does not think she can succeed and/or she is just not interested in the topic.

My husband is an electrical engineer. Yet whenever he volunteers information about electricity to Susan, she sets her face and no amount of cajoling will induce her to listen. She must freely come to him for the information she seeks. She prefers to search out her own answers in her own way. Of our three youngsters, she is the one most likely to adamantly refuse to proceed unless she feels confident of success and the one who prefers to find her own answers without assistance.

One May we planned to drive to Minnesota to visit grandparents. In March I gave each child a map to plot out the route we'd take. All I specified was that it had to be completed in three weeks, at least five days were to be at their grandparents', and we would travel no more than 450 miles in a given day. Even Dale and I plotted out our plans. Then we compared our maps to come up with a final itinerary.

Once the route was settled upon, each child chose which state tourism office to write for further information. They also wrote to the chambers of commerce in selected cities for motel information. We studied information from the American Automobile Association. Beautiful tourism materials arrived and as it did we started noticing things of historical interest, such as the wagon trails through Nebraska and Wyoming.

With tourism materials in hand we decided where to concentrate our time during this trip. Going to Minnesota, we spent extra time at the Grand Canyon and in the Colorado Rockies. Leaving Minnesota, we stayed five days in the Rapid City area of South Dakota visiting the Badlands, viewing Mount Rushmore and the Crazy Horse Memorial, and exploring the depths of nearby caves.

Because they were actively involved in the planning, we had a delightful trip. We did not try to see and do everything so that we could enjoy ourselves. There will be other opportunities to see and do what we missed the first time if it is important enough to us.

Two years after the trip they still mention things learned on that trip. What better way to grasp the enormity of a buffalo than to have to stop the car so one can amble across the road right in front of you in Wind Cave National Park? Going along the Platte River for so many miles we tried to imagine the wagon trains going westward without the benefit of freeways. Visiting Crazy Horse Memorial sparked more than a passing interest in the plight of our American Indians.

The ever changing scenery changed their concept of our American desert through California and Arizona. Finally, leaving relatives in Carson City, Nevada, we travelled Highway 88 over Kit Carson Pass. Jim marvelled, "Mom, I had no idea California had scenery as spectacular as the Rockies." (Something I took for granted as I have often been to the Sierra Nevada and suddenly realized our youngsters hadn't.)

When Jim won the essay contest that took the family to Washington, D.C., I remember one of the other winners, a high school senior. We were almost done with a tour of the White House when he stood looking in awe at one of the many paintings decorating the White House. He commented, "These are *real* paintings! I've seen them so many times in my history and American Government text books, but I never realized they were anything more than a picture in a book." The next day as we were finishing up our last tour as a group, this young man told me that now U. S. history made sense to him. It really happened. He was standing where it happened. From then on it would mean so much more to him.

Ever since that trip four years ago, Jim and Laurie watch the news with interest when scenes of places they visited on that trip are shown. Susan does not remember as much, although she does remember being in the Washington Monument. Just knowing that she was in those historical places is important to her though. United States history is more interesting because of this trip.

Our youngsters read the newspaper daily. Jim

usually reads it while rolling his papers for delivery. They each have their favorite parts and all agree on the comics page. Laurie even wrote a letter of protest when they dropped the cartoon, *Marmaduke*. (I knew nothing about that letter until it appeared in the "Letters to the Editor" along with an apology from the paper with a promise to reinstate *Marmaduke* due to popular outcry.) But sometime during the month they have read each section of the paper.

According to the varying interests of the family, we subscribe to several different magazines. The periodicals change as our interests change. Jim reads *Sports Illustrated* practically from cover to cover. If he could afford to he would subscribe to *The Wall Street Journal* and *USA Today*. Laurie loves *Kid City* (which used to be called *Electric Company*). Susan's favorite is *Ranger Rick*.

The universal favorite magazine in our family is *Reader's Digest*. Being avid comparison shoppers all three kids love *Zillions*. We also have several computer magazines around. There are many more we like to read, but there are only so many hours a day and so much money available for subscriptions.

By far, *Reader's Digest* has stimulated the most learning experiences. One day Susan started discussing viruses, what they are, what they do, what scientists know about them. At first I was puzzled as to where she had come upon that information.

Then she told me she had been in her room reading a back issue of *Reader's Digest*. There is such a broad variety of topics covered in this magazine. The youngsters are exposed to many different subjects while reading it.

The "Spin Off" pages in *Gifted Children Monthly* provide many opportunities for interesting activities. The games and puzzles intrigue the children. Jim has participated in their surveys and obtained several pen pals. Susan won a book and had her Constitutional Bicentennial poster published in "Spin Off." Laurie has been chosen as a Student Advisor for a year because of an essay she wrote.

Dale is an amateur radio operator and involved in local emergency preparedness. His interest in ham radio was sparked as a young teenager and has been a lifelong source of enjoyment for him. For a while Jim showed some interest in being one also, but that interest has died down. While Dale would love to share his interest with the youngsters, he also recognizes that, at least for now, none of them are likely to take up this hobby.

I have edited many different newsletters. The youngsters have grown up watching me do this and assisting me with the newsletters. How much this has influenced Laurie I do not know as she claims that editing her own newsletter was entirely her own idea.

She started her own newsletter, *Monthly Star*, two years ago and has kept it going despite not receiving the input from other young writers that she expected. In addition she and her friends Missy and Sabrina co-edited a joint effort called *Kids Monthly*. I do not enter into any part of the editing unless I'm specifically asked. At first I offered suggestions but was told in no uncertain terms that this was her project and when she wanted help, she'd ask for it.

Jim and Susan also tried their hand at editing their own newsletters. Susan's abiding interest is science so she entitled hers *Sleepover Science*. Jim's reflected his interest in baseball. Their endeavors only lasted for two issues but they received a positive reaction from their readers.

In my efforts to encourage their writing skills through actual writing exercises, I quickly learned that unless it is a project in which they have a special interest my urgings are usually ignored. Sometimes they give an outright refusal to participate in a project. Many times they will halfheartedly go along with my project, and it is obvious that they are only doing it to please me. Yet when I least expect it they can produce a high quality piece of writing even if I am in a state of despair of their ever writing anything I consider worthwhile. It comes down to a definition of "worthwhile." Is it worthwhile to me or to them? If it is worthwhile to them they produce a written piece that many times is quite impressive. This often occurs after a lengthy period of writing barrenness.

Herb Hammer introduced Jim, Laurie, and Susan to an interactive public radio program for youngsters called *Kids America*. Since we could not receive the program on our public radio station, he taped the 90 minute program each weekday for us. The live program originated in New York. Youngsters could use an 800 number to call in live responses to the program.

Even though we listened to the program on a delayed basis, Jim and Laurie did call and were on the program several times. Jim introduced the song of the week on his birthday on the air. Laurie stumped the show's spelling wiz and won a book for her efforts. She also received a book from Dr. Book when she suggested an interesting book to listeners. Both youngsters were delighted to hear themselves on the radio thanks to Herb taping the show. They would have participated in other segments of the program such as the geography treasure hunts if we were able to listen to the program live.

Laurie participated in their joint project with Kodak and the publishers of the book <u>Christmas in America</u>. Kodak provided two rolls of 36 exposure 135 film, and the youngsters took pictures of Christmas activities to submit. The publishers selected some of the pictures for inclusion in their book. Laurie learned that when you commit to a project you see it to the end even when the project becomes tedious. She found having to record the event and identifying all the participants in each picture tiresome by the time she was shooting her second roll of film.

Due to lack of adequate funding for *Kids America* the program is no longer broadcast. But Jim and Laurie worked up a petition to our local public radio station in an effort to save the program. They also wrote letters to various home school newsletters and magazines encouraging families to join their effort to save the program. This written project was all of their own doing and I was impressed with their efforts. It had meaning to them, and they produced well thought out and grammatically superb letters without much assistance from me.

One nice spring day we noticed electric company linemen changing the configuration of the poles on the hill above us. We knew about the red tail hawk nest on the pole closest to us. Laurie and I watched fascinated while five men carefully brought down the nest with two chicks and three eggs. They built a new platform for the nest about halfway up the pole, then returned the nest to the pole. Acoustics were excellent so we heard everything the men said even though the distance from us was great. In their concern for the nesting parents, the linemen left the site for five hours. Laurie and I rejoiced as the parents circled and finally landed on their new nesting site.

Later in the day Laurie sat down at the typewriter and wrote a report on what we had witnessed. I had no idea at the time what she was typing. She then submitted her story to *Home Education Magazine* and was thrilled when they published it. Had I told her to sit down and write this report, I know without any doubt that she would have resisted. Even if she had done it to please me, I do not think it would have been as well written.

One time Laurie did ask me, in fact begged me, to assign a special report to her about some aspect of American history. We came up with a mutually acceptable topic but that was as far as the report went. She had lost interest in the subject. I could have held her to the report, but it would have become a struggle and no educational advantage would have been attained.

Another time we were doing a joint study of American Indian tribes using a specifically marked U. S. map. Laurie asked me for a blank U. S. map as she wanted to see if she could still identify all the states. Two of the New England states gave her a problem but she found her way using a road atlas. Finding her own answers gave her a sense of satisfaction and helped impress upon her the relationship of our various states.

For this reason I have numerous blank maps of every region of the world which the youngsters are free to use when and how they please. During the Olympics these maps were used almost daily. Susan's favorite maps are those with mileage distances as she loves to calculate distances. At first I could only locate blank maps to copy on spirit duplicators (we had a friend with one available so that was no real problem). We no longer have that resource, but in the meantime I found some excellent blackline maps in the Good Year Education series book, The Map Corner, published by Scott, Foresman and Company.

Home Education Magazine and *Growing Without Schooling* contain many first hand stories about how trusting children to learn what is needed when it is needed is rewarded by eagerness to learn even more all the time. Repeatedly you read of incidents that the amount learned was related to how the student felt about her ability to accomplish the work.

When the parents allowed the student to use her abilities according to her interests, she learned more and retained this knowledge. *Home Education Magazine* compiled some of these stories in their excellent book, The Home School Reader.

David and Micki Colfax are well known as parents of the outstanding scholars Grant and Drew. They began home schooling because they were concerned that their boys would lose a love for learning and exploration. In their book, Homeschooling for Excellence, they emphasize the necessity of providing our youngsters with the tools for learning and then letting the student take control of the direction of learning.

John Holt wrote several books in which he constantly emphasized the necessity of trusting our children to choose wisely. He claimed that if we give a student the opportunity, she will make better sense of the world than if she is constantly told what is best for her.

One summer day as I was hanging clothes on the line Susan was nearby studying the local crawling creatures. She dearly loves to be outdoors observing nature closely. She was holding a science textbook in her hands. Looking up at me she said, "I like to learn by teaching myself. I don't like someone else to teach me because I learn better by teaching myself."

Being in a classroom frustrated her because she never felt she had enough time to pursue her studies in her own way and often had to waste time waiting for her classmates to finish up a project so she could go on. She told my husband and me, "School puts too much pressure on me. It makes me feel hot all over and uncomfortable. At school I can't learn what I want to when I want to."

Often Susan will play with her dolls and have lively conversations with them. After one particularly lengthy session during which I overheard her making many remarks about geography, she looked over at me and explained that this is her favorite way to learn something. Acting it out with her dolls impresses it on her mind. She also hastened to add that she liked to have her home school friends over for the same reason. With her friends she is able to have interactive learning.

Shortly after I had started home schooling, I wrote to a friend: *At first I was puzzled by "motivation" battles I had with Jim and Laurie which always resolved themselves in surprising ways. After one such incident I really had doubts about what was happening to Jim and Laurie. But the last couple of days they have really astounded me with their activities. Jim has been willingly working in his algebra book and Laurie picked up a couple of math booklets I found at the textbook center but did not think either one would be that interested in. She found several projects which she became engrossed in. One was making geometrical shapes and boxes out of paper. Both of them conducted separate crystal garden experiments without any prompting from me yesterday.*

With the passage of time this anxiety has eased. I see how many ways there are to indicate a growth in learning. My file cabinet is filled with examples of their creativity and projects. I realize I had unrealistic expectations. My youngsters are ordinary youngsters, yet I was expecting extraordinary feats. When we are relaxed, learning abounds; but when I am anxious about progress very little is accomplished. The biggest lesson has been to accept each child for who she is and myself as I am. Trust is not static. It changes with circumstances so I must also change and allow my students to change. What worked yesterday will not necessarily work today.

There certainly are days when I question what is taking place. While the youngsters are doing very well, I am the one feeling pressured to get them to perform some externally measurable school work. There is that nagging worry about someone demanding to see proof acceptable to them that learning is taking place. I personally see invaluable learning occurring but still worry that it is acceptable to "others," whoever "they" are.

My children need to know that I have confidence in them in their quest for knowledge. In my own efforts to learn to use a computer I quickly retreat whenever I lack confidence in myself. I am influenced by what I perceive others think of me. I have to remind myself that it is okay to feel uncertain of myself. I am the one who has to choose to rise above my current level of ability.

My years of experience with life spans many more years than those of my children. I know from experience that the struggle to master the computer is worthwhile. I consider it my responsibility to inspire similar confidence in my children so that they, too, can expand their horizons.

I will not inspire this confidence if I am their judge and their manipulator. I want to encourage their efforts in problem solving and thinking skills. This includes nurturing their interests and respecting their capability to decide what is of importance to them. They do not need to compare themselves to others. First I want to instill in them a feeling of competence and self-worth.

A remedial reading teacher, Ellen Brandoff Matter, wrote an article in *Learning 88* describing her experience with a wood working class offered at an adult night school. She wanted to make a six foot cabinet that would fit in her dining room. It was an ambitious undertaking for a beginner. During the construction phase she had to overcome many frustrations and misunderstandings as to how to proceed. The finished product was far from perfect but she was proud of her accomplishment. Because of this experience she began to appreciate what her students face on a daily basis as they are asked to learn new skills. Her comment was, "By becoming a student again, I got a chance to walk in my students' shoes -- and ended up with blisters."

As I read her article I mentally compared my experiences in learning how to use this computer and word processing program to how my children learn. At first I doubted I could ever learn to use the computer. It seemed so complicated. I could hardly understand the manuals, and when I asked questions about the computer the answers I received sounded like they were in a foreign language. The demonstration disks did not help me that much as I preferred to start out on a "real" project.

The books, manuals and instructors I questioned assumed I knew more than I did. For instance, it took me many months to figure out why I could not get my sequential page numbers to print. In the meantime I avoided using page numbers or else used the typewriter to put them in place. This was tedious. One day, quite by accident, I happened to read one vital sentence buried in a place that I did not expect to find it. I had been putting the correct codes in but was also unknowingly cancelling out the codes by one simple keystroke.

We do our youngsters a disservice by introducing them to grades and testing before they are ready. Letter grades on the elementary level are irrelevant and can be detrimental. This is the time to concentrate on learning the basic skills and laying a firm foundation for the future. With sadness I watched some youngsters fall behind in the first grade when I was a classroom volunteer and had the time to closely observe what was taking place. As I followed their progress, several of them became used to receiving low grades and could not catch up to their classmates later on.

Seeing no educational value in giving grades on work accomplished, I do not grade my youngsters. They and I know without any doubt how they are performing. When they experience a problem we work it out. Sometimes it means dropping a project temporarily until that child is ready to proceed.

Other times it is apparent the topic was inappropriate for that particular child. I am not placed in the position of a judge and they are not being judged by anyone other than themselves.

What real purpose do letter grades serve? My grades in high school have had little influence on my lifetime activities. Going to several of my high school reunions I noticed that academic success was not recognized. My classmates who excelled in sports or social skills were given recognition during the festivities.

During my studies at junior college I participated in an interesting experiment. Students were expected to do their best but were not told what their final grades were. I felt freer to pursue my interests in my studies without worrying about my grades. Only when I enrolled in the University of San Francisco three years later did I learn of my final grades, which were right where I expected them to be.

This experiment influences me today. I don't grade my youngsters' work unless it is required by an outside agency. When it is necessary, I point out to my youngsters that this is my assessment of their work but they know themselves better than anyone else can, including their mother.

Testing is another matter that requires consideration. Studies show it can be detrimental. What positive value does testing have? Standardized tests do not measure what they claim to measure. They are biased and have long term negative effects on students, especially creative thinkers, minorities, women, and anyone who does not possess the same values or experiences as the testmakers.

Standardized tests are a vote of "no confidence" in the learner. If you are confident that a student knows something, you do not need to test her. She wants to please adults so she takes the tests, then considers herself a failure despite the wrongness of the test for her. Standardized tests interfere with learning by fostering the use of a standardized curriculum or else requiring that hours be spent preparing for and taking these tests.

My youngsters took many standardized tests during their years in public school. I assisted in administering tests several times so can appreciate the amount of time during the school year devoted to taking these tests that could be more productively spent on interesting projects. Conditions for the testing are not always ideal, either. I've administered some of the tests in a crowded janitor's equipment room and also in the classroom where someone was constantly coming to the door or the intercom was active. James R. Delisle, Ph. D., answered a parent's question on standardized tests and test anxiety in *Gifted Children Monthly* by commenting that all too often these tests are administered under conditions that cause anxiety in even the most relaxed student, yet we expect optimal performance.

Susan was in a school that was part of the Chapter One program to offer slower students personal remedial help. We do not know what happened the day she took the test with all her kindergarten classmates, but the results showed she was in great need of remedial attention. This is a child who excels academically. It turned out to her advantage as she was entitled to independent study projects very much to her liking, but in another school where I also volunteered she would have come away feeling incompetent.

One time I obtained copies of standardized tests. When I showed them to Jim, Laurie, and Susan they let out a collective groan and expressed strong distaste. At my insistence, they did consent to taking them. When we went through the results I found that they were right where I observed from their work that they would be in each academic area. What was particularly fascinating was discussing their reasons for choosing "wrong" answers. In each case they could come up with a valid reason for choosing the answer they did. Their reasons, in my opinion, were more valid than the "right" answers.

I encourage every parent unacquainted with standardized tests to obtain copies of them. This removes the mystery that surrounds testing for parents unacquainted with the content of these tests. Standardized testing has become a fact of life. Until the movement to reduce the status of testing strengthens it is important for us to become more aware of the facts about standardized testing.

Testing is an effective means of control. If a student is to perform well on a standardized test, the curriculum needs to be geared to the tests. This assumes that a school choses a standardized test and then chooses a curriculum that prepares the student to pass it. The student's interests, aptitudes, abilities, and needs are not taken into account. The goal of learning thus becomes to pass the test, not to acquire lifelong skills and a love for learning.

The Friends of Education from the state of West Virginia announced the results of their survey on standardized testing in newspapers throughout the nation in November, 1987. *Gifted Children Monthly* wrote a review of the article from *The New York Times*. Their finding was that no state is below the average at the elementary level in the six major nationally normed commercially available tests.

How could that be since "average" assumes that someone has to be below and someone has to be above the average, they asked. These 1987 students were compared to out of date norms. Schools were teaching to the test by tailoring curriculum to increase test scores. The Friends of Education group warned that in order to find the time to teach to the test, you have to take away time from enrichment activities, independent projects, and accelerated learning.

Bruce McGill, president of Educational Records Bureau, a Wellesley, Massachusetts based testing organization used by many top private and public college preparatory schools, praises the Friends of Education analysis and adds another reason for the unrealistically high test results. He states that the tests are geared for all students and all kinds of schools therefore the tests don't have enough difficult questions to challenge 25 to 30% of the students taking the tests.

The reviewer noted that several publishers of

the tests were reluctant to revise the tests because of the great expense involved. It would require hours of additional testing of hundreds of thousands of students. Because of the concerns raised by the Friends of Education, the publishers of the Iowa Test, the California Test of Basic Skills, and the California Achievement Test are in the process of updating their norms. The other tests involved in the Friends study are the Stanford Achievement Test, the Metropolitan Achievement Test, and the Science Research Achievement Test.

Gifted Children Monthly also reviewed *Beyond Standardized Tests: Admission Alternatives That Work*, a publication from the National Center for Fair and Open Testing (FairTest). They provided a list of colleges and graduate schools dropping or deemphasizing standard admission exams. The reasons given for dropping the exams were unfair biases against women and minorities, distortions due to pre-test coaching, and the impact of tests on curriculum and self-esteem. Among those dropping the exams were Harvard Business School, Johns Hopkins Medical School, and the Massachusetts Institute of Technology.

James Alvino, editor of *Gifted Children Monthly*, states that the Educational Testing Service developed the SAT to measure *developed* abilities rather than innate abilities of high school students. This was to be a tool to predict the student's success in her freshman year of college. The test may measure what he labels "school house smarts" but fails to measure any creative or practical abilities needed for success in life.

There are several books about the harmful effects testing can have upon students. One of these that I have read is <u>None of the Above: Behind the Myth of Scholastic Aptitude</u>, by David Owen. The theme of this book is to debunk the mythology surrounding standardized testing. He claims that we defer to the tests because we *think* the tests see what we cannot. We have ascribed power to testing that is out of proportion to the actual content. This allows the sense of insecurity to overcome the test takers. We tend to be better at concocting excuses for giving tests than we are at making sense of the results of the tests. Most of the book is about the SAT, but he does cover test making and test taking in general. Often we hear American children compared to Japanese children. David Owen addresses that issue by showing how testing determines the Japanese educational fate without instilling a lifelong love for learning.

Frank Smith wrote in <u>Insult to Intelligence</u> that systematic testing has its roots in Britain during the early years of this century. He claims it was closely linked with the influential eugenics movement seeking to breed an intellectual elite. Cyril Burt, a psychology professor knighted for his service as a designer of mental and scholastic tests was convinced that the intelligence his tests measured was inherited. Eventually he was discredited when it was learned he had faked his data, but not before the damage was done.

Psychology gained its hold over education

through the testing movement. Initially psychologists needed educational data for their own research, but gradually test results were used to make educational decisions. Until recently educational research has been almost entirely a matter of testing children, but some researchers are now probing the classroom environment and the behavior of teachers as well. Standardized tests promise to lead to improvement in educational practices and teaching, yet data gathered from schools suggests otherwise. The Center for the Evaluation of Data at UCLA conducted a five year survey of test use. The conclusion they arrived at was that school personnel give more weight to teachers' judgements than to information from mandated standardized tests. Teachers felt they had a better feel for students' strengths and weaknesses from their own observations and measures.

I think it is important to consider carefully when deciding the value and goal of testing. There are other means at our disposal for measuring educational progress. One way I use is to establish general learning goals and objectives for each child, keeping records on progress, and assessing the progress by observation and periodic reviews. This takes into account many more of the student's abilities, and does not have the problems associated with standardized testing. It becomes a much more realistic view of the learning that has and is taking place. Learning in this manner stays with the student longer. How often we deplore students learning something for a test and then promptly forgetting it when testing is over.

Trust. A small word with an enormous meaning. Learning is based on trust. We are always learning. Learning does not require coercion or irrelevant reward. Our children deserve our trust. A child learns best when she understands what she learns and how it affects her personally. Most learning is incidental because the child learns as she is doing things she finds useful and interesting. Learning is collaborative and it is defeated when instruction is delivered mechanically. A student demonstrates the worthwhile things she has learned by engaging in related activities, and she should not have to rely on grades, scores, or tests. Learning involves feelings. She will remember how she felt when she learned -- and when she failed to learn.

Until we can accept that the human mind remains a mystery, we operate under the delusion that it is possible to know, measure, and control what goes on in our childrens' minds. Possibly "control" is the key to why so many adults have a problem accepting the fact that children learn much more through interest initiated learning than through other directed learning.

CHAPTER FIVE

KEEPING FUTURE EDUCATIONAL OPPORTUNITIES OPEN

Friends and acquaintances looked at us with raised eyebrows and puzzled looks on their faces when they saw my husband and I attending the special meeting for incoming freshmen at our public high school. What were we doing there? You could see the thoughts parade across their faces. Maybe we had finally come to our senses regarding schools. Some showed shock that we had changed our minds. Various fleeting emotions flashed in their eyes. Mostly we were just greeted with looks of surprise.

We were singled out because we had chosen to home school for awhile. In our town it is assumed that students will attend public school. A few attend small private schools. Many parents are unaware of the varied educational opportunities that are available.

Jim personally chose to enter the public high school. He now feels that he has control over his education and is making some wise choices. During Back to School Night, his teachers told us how much they enjoyed having Jim in their classes because he is so interested in learning and because of his meaningful participation in the classroom.

He has a good relationship with his peers and his teachers. He wants to be in his classes so there is now no struggle to get up in the morning as there used to be. The pressures he had been under in earlier years no longer are there so he can now develop healthy peer relationships. Homework is promptly completed. He was even able to tolerate a boring social studies teacher. Jim no longer feels trapped because he realized that he does have other options open. He has the freedom of choice.

Every year the high school anticipates difficulties with the incoming freshmen who had been at the local middle school. The majority of students come to high school from a closed campus where all the gates lock them in for the school day with the exception of an open gate by the administrative office. There are very strict rules on campus to curb violence that occurs. Their day is regimented. They cannot leave campus without compelling reason. Then they go to the high school which is a completely open campus and have an hour long lunch period. They may leave campus at any time during the day (assuming they do not have a class that period). Many students have problems with their relative freedom of choice for the first several weeks. This year there were more problems than usual. Jim had no difficulty adjusting to his schedule since he had just come from an environment of choice.

Enrolling Jim proved to have unexpected advantages. Incoming students not from local public or private schools must register just a few days before the start of school. Most incoming students do not get to personally meet their counselor prior to some problem. Jim and I had to see his assigned counselor for the enrollment process. We discussed what subjects Jim had studied at home.

On the strength of our discussion his counselor placed him with excellent teachers (with one exception, but according to Jim the other teacher was worse). The counselor signed him up for advanced computers and for geometry. These courses had a prerequisite of algebra I so most freshmen are ineligible. The counselor looked at Jim's algebra book and was satisfied. Later on Jim was placed in Honors geometry.

What Jim's future holds now depends on him. He knows he has choices. It is up to him to research these choices to find the ones which will equip him with the skills he wants. His father and I are here to provide him with information and insight when he wishes. He needs to discover on his own what contributions he wants to make to society. We have tried to provide the atmosphere that promotes excitement in him for learning all he can.

To address this issue, the editors of *Home Ed-*

ucation Magazine, Mark and Helen Hegener, published a book, <u>Alternatives in Education</u>. The editors of *Gifted Children Monthly* considered this such a valuable book that they have included it in their highly selective catalog, Presents for the Promising. Topics include the meaning of alternative education and many of the options available to parents and students. Various alternative educators' philosophies are succinctly discussed. A chapter is devoted to home schooling but most of the book reminds the reader that we do have many educational options available to us. It is up to the individuals involved to explore these possibilities for the most suitable program.

Thomas Kane home schooled until he entered the University of Maine where he maintained a triple major of science, foreign policy, and writing. He entered the University at the age of 14 and encountered no difficulties because of his age. However, he noticed a girl his age did encounter problems because she looked more her age than he did. His experience with his professors was positive because they were delighted to have a student more interested in learning than in "grades". He voices a common complaint among high school students when he notes that many students are capable of graduating long before traditional schools let them.

The major consideration in looking at educational alternatives is to find the option in which the student will succeed. The learning style as well as the interests of the student is important. It is not the student who fails so much as it is the student being placed in a situation that is not right for her.

Christopher Hurn, from the University of Massachusetts, devotes his sociology textbook, The Limits and Possibilities of Schooling: An Introduction to the Sociology of Education, to the premise that American schooling cannot change until people are willing to let go of the status quo. Competition for the top jobs and status makes it difficult to risk losing a person's spot on the social scale to someone perceived as an inferior.

Shortly after we brought Jim home for his studies, I attended PTA council meetings as an officer of the board. The outgoing president remained on the board and never hesitated to speak forcefully on any issue that came up. Someone mentioned the local continuation high school for troubled teenagers. She thought the very idea of a continuation school alternative was abhorrent. Her main concern was that it was unfair to her own youngsters because they had to go all four years to high school while these youngsters could obtain their high school diploma in less time and with less work. She cited cases where some able students had deliberately misbehaved so that they would be sent to Maple High School to finish their high school early. She successfully did all she could to dissuade the school district in attempts to begin an Independent Study Program. In this she had allies among some of the district administrators and teachers as well as other parents.

Tyra Seymour, a fifteen year veteran teacher/ coordinator for the School Within a School at J.F.K.

High School in Los Angeles, wrote of her increasing frustration with the educational community's inability to accept any differences in schooling practices. She asked support from the National Coalition of Alternative Schools in her article for their newsletter. Recent California reforms have moved school districts toward greater uniformity and conformity. We live in a country that professes freedom of choice and uniqueness. The program salvaged students who could have otherwise been lost to society. Graduates continually write or personally return to thank their teachers for turning them back on to learning and even on to themselves.

The College of Creative Studies at the University of California Santa Barbara has its share of critics who constantly attempt to undermine it because it does not conform to preconceived ideas of education and control over students. Colleges and universities offering Independent Study Programs also face this opposition.

Columbia Pacific University sends a reprint of an article that appeared in The Chronicle of Higher Education to prospective students in their Independent Study Program. Michael Beaudoin, dean of continuing education and external degree programs at Saint Joseph's College in Maine, agrees that there is much prejudice against academic programs not conforming precisely to the curriculum for full-time students. Skepticism remains despite the fact that home study has successfully existed for hundreds of years. He notes that some of the most ardent opponents to alternative education through independent

study often have vested interests in classroom instruction.

Educational options exist. Opposition to
many of these options also exists. Knowledge about
the opposition and the reasons behind opposition
forces us to be more aware of our own educational
goals for ourselves and our students.

We chose the educational option of home
schooling our three youngsters primarily because
we want them to have a life long love of learning
and to feel good about their ability to learn. We recognized that each of them had their own approach
to learning. Each youngster has rewarded our faith
in them to choose wisely what is of importance to
them. At no time do we want to close any other educational options, though. We continually reassess
their progress and their needs. And we expect to
make mistakes, but we also expect to learn from
these errors in judgement.

Brian Ray, Ph. D. presented a paper, *A Comparison of Home Schooling and Conventional
Schooling: With a Focus on Learner Outcomes in
1987* in which he reviewed relevant literature.
Summarizing what other researchers had found, he
concluded that home schooled students benefit
enormously from the low student-teacher ratio and
the high involvement of the parents in the learning
process. The extra attention afforded by the parents
may raise the child's self concept which in turn is
associated with improved learning.

Because the parents tend to have higher expectations of their children, greater academic perfor-

mance may result. Home schooling is frequently involved in learning within the frame work of daily
living activities. This promotes active involvement
in learning by discovery. In terms of curriculum,
home schooling lends itself to a high degree of indi-
vidualization and flexibility. He notes that parents
who home school frequently exhibit the behaviors
consistent with teacher effectiveness such as flexibility, enthusiasm, task orientation, and clarity of organization.

As we have home schooled, I have personally
witnessed the benefits as outlined by Brian Ray not
only in our family but also in other home schooling
families. We have the time to offer our students
that no teacher in a conventional classroom situation has. Due to financing I have watched the teach-
er/student ratio climb in our school district despite
efforts to lower it. I watched teacher enthusiasm
wane in our neighborhood school when an inept
principal was appointed. I felt I had something better to offer my youngsters for as long as they desired
and needed it. This is the option we choose for
now.

Besides his dissertation on learner outcomes
of home schooling, Brian Ray has produced a
lengthy home-centered learning annotated bibliog-
raphy with over 350 entries covering relevant research. He also edits a quarterly publication, *Home
School Researcher*, as a means of sharing the latest
research available pertaining to home schooling.
The June, 1988, issue contained two articles relating
to research into the amount of structure used in

homeschooling and the effect on achievement.

Sonia Gustafson is at the Woodrow Wilson School of Public and International Affairs in Princeton University. Her project involved exploring the motivation and goals of home schooling parents through a survey of families listed in the publication *Growing Without Schooling*. Of the 143 respondents she found that 65% of the families used highly informal or flexible structures. Only 30% indicated formal instruction. Most families stated that flexibility was more important to them than formal lessons or schedules. They placed more value on "teachable moments" no matter when or where they occur than on a required number of academic exercises in a given day.

She adds that parents who responded to her survey exhibited a fierce devotion to providing an educational environment which offer their children the opportunity to develop freely and fully in more than academic areas. They consider it important to develop all areas of being. She also noted that the parents whose children had taken standardized tests reported the students had scored above average.

Jon Wartes, Project Leader for the Washington Homeschool Research Project, reported on the results of home school testing using the Stanford Achievement Test. His finding was that the test data suggested there is virtually no relationship between the level of structure used and the academic outcome. The level of structure used had no value in predicting the outcome of test scores. There seems to be no support for imposing curriculum for the sake of structure nor for imposing minimum hours per week of formal schooling.

It is interesting to note that Jon Wartes, a public school administrator in the state of Washington, readily admits that at first he was opposed to home schooling because he was convinced quality education requires highly trained teachers. He wanted to protect teachers, funding, and the imposition of a particular philosophy on students. Once he was convinced that home schooling is a viable option, he became a proponent of the movement.

In an article in *Growing Without Schooling*, he cautions home schoolers not to claim academic superiority when dealing with school administrators. While there is evidence that support the claim, too many important variables have not yet been controlled in the research conducted to date. This is one of the reasons he is working so closely with the project in the state of Washington where similar groups of public school students and home school students in the same locality are being studied.

The question of teacher certification is of importance to parents who choose to home school their youngsters. Teacher certification is supposed to be a guarantee of educational quality and the capability of the person to teach students. If teacher certification is the means to assure quality education, why can't the various states agree on a nationally uniform course of study and standard means of evaluation of who is qualified to teach?

My cousin cannot teach in California public

schools because her certification is from Oregon and my sister-in-law cannot teach in Oregon because her certification is from the state of Washington. We probably all know someone who is eminently qualified to teach but unable to in the state where he or she now resides because that state does not recognize their teaching credentials.

Dr. Sam Peavey, Professor Emeritus of Education at the University of Louisville, was actively involved for years in training new teachers. Yet he admits that half a century of research has failed to prove there is significant relationship between teacher certification and student achievement. He considers the only valid measure of teacher effectiveness is learner achievement.

Another concern for some parents who believe in student initiated learning is will their children be able to handle post secondary studies. Depending on the individual student, there seems to be no particular problem with higher studies. In fact, some students have reported that their college and university experiences were enriched because they were more interested in learning than in their grades. College admission seems to pose no more problems for home schooled youngsters than those entering out of public schools. There may be a variation in the manner of applying for admission to the college or university of choice, though.

In most cases the student should be prepared to take some standardized tests such as the SAT. If those scores are high there usually is no problem. If the scores are average or low there will probably be an interview, the need for references, and samples of essay writing abilities. However, you won't know what to expect until you apply to a specific college or university.

Brian Ray reviewed a study made of university admissions requirements for home schooled applicants. The researcher was Leslie Barnebey who did her doctoral dissertation on this topic. The study showed that private universities were more likely to accept home schooled applicants than the public universities were. Home schoolers are more often required to submit letters of reference, essays, and Achievement Test scores. Almost 84% of the accepting colleges and universities accepted the GED in lieu of high school transcripts. Many of the colleges and universities encouraged prior attendance at junior or community colleges. Three quarters of the accepting colleges believed that home schooled applicants would be successful as other applicants. Nearly all of the colleges and universities surveyed (91%) do not have a formal policy regarding home school applicants. In conclusion, home schooled students are accepted into a wide range of four year universities and colleges, especially the large, private, research oriented universities.

As home schooling parents, we wonder whether our children will be penalized when seeking college admission if their high school program is not accredited. My research into the question reveals that accreditation is not an indication of the legal status of the school, but of its acceptability to the standards of a recognized accrediting agency. These

are independent accrediting organizations who usually charge for this service and have varying standards. Schools can be perfectly legal and the work of
their students can be accepted by other schools and
colleges without ever being accredited.

The significance of accreditation depends on
the student's plans for the immediate future. Accreditation has no meaning at all if the student's
plans do not include college, but rather getting a job
after graduation. If the student wants to attend a
college or university immediately after graduation,
accreditation can enter the picture. At times it does
play a part in the selection process at competitive
four year universities. On the other hand, hundreds of colleges throughout the nation accept diplo-
mas from non-accredited high schools without any
difficulty at all. If a student has a particular career
goal in mind, it is wise to investigate the requirements early. Entering college after several years in
the work force seems to pose little problem.

Generally, college and university admission
standards are becoming more flexible. The key element which they often rely upon at present seems
to be the SAT scores. With favorable test scores
even competitive four year colleges and universities
will often accept a student, regardless of attendance
at an accredited school, a non-accredited school, or
even no school at all.

A high school diploma or its equivalent is almost a necessity in the job market. There are some
jobs available where it is not required but usually
these are low-paying and there is no advancement

without the diploma. California provides the California High School Proficiency Examination which is accepted in the state as the equivalent to a high school diploma.

The General Educational Development Test, or GED, is a more widely accepted high school diploma equivalent. Originally designed during World War II to allow veterans to go to college without returning to high school to finish secondary courses, the GED is used for purposes of higher education, employment, promotion, and licensing. The age and residence requirements vary from the state, territory, district, or Canadian province, in which the test is taken. The purpose is to measure the skills mastered and general knowledge that would be acquired in a four year high school education. There are many books available in libraries and bookstores to assist in preparation for the test.

National attention has been focused in recent years on the academic achievements of the Colfax family. They are examples of the educational heights that can be achieved by home schooled youngsters. During an interview on the Phil Donahue program the parents emphasized that most of the learning was unassisted by them. While the boys were encouraged to spend at least twenty minutes a day on basic subjects, there was no pressure to do so. Never were they forced to spend several hours a day on studies.

Another former home schooler, John Wesley Taylor V, based his doctoral dissertation on the self-concept of home schooled children. His findings showed that the self-concept of the home schooled children studied was significantly higher than that of conventionally schooled children. He concludes that this may be due to higher achievement and mastery levels. Other factors are the independent study characteristics and tutoring situations found in the home school environment. Higher levels of parental involvement, independence from peers, a sense of responsibility and lower anxiety levels are other factors he considers important.

John Wesley Taylor began his home schooling at the age of eight. His family was in Latin America at the time he began home schooling. During the ninth to twelfth grade he studied on his own using Home Study International courses. He remembers this as a time to follow his own interests and for community service. At the age of eighteen he entered college where he became interested in the field of education. He currently is on the faculty of Andrews University, having obtained his Ph.D. in Curriculum and Instruction.

John Boston is the administrator for Home Centered Learning. His philosophy is one which he calls "invited teaching" which he defines as helping someone else when they ask for help. As word has spread of his encouragement of student initiated learning, his enrollment has doubled in one year's time to nearly 300 students by the end of 1988. In his home schooling program he encourages parents to communicate with their students so that the student's needs are accurately assessed. A former public high school teacher himself, he no longer believes that the best situation for learning can be guessed at by a curriculum developer. The educational needs of his own son compelled him to found the School of Home Learning as he discovered other parents with similar experiences.

Sean Boston was one of the first graduates from the School of Home Learning. Since then twenty-one other students have joined the ranks of School of Home Learning alumni. I wrote to several of them explaining my book on the value of allowing students to follow their interests during the learning process. Then I asked them to share their comments.

Heather finished high school at home after getting into trouble at the public high school. Her highlights in home schooling were time to read and other quiet "productive" times. She began to understand balancing a checkbook. She planned to take courses on becoming a medical or dental receptionist until she eloped and became pregnant. She cherishes her time to write fiction and even had a book accepted for publication at the age of 15. When asked what she would tell teachers about effective teaching she mentioned she'd stress individual attention, praise for a job well done and to let students do it at their own pace.

Diana wrote a lengthy reply to my letter. She home schooled for six years (from the fourth grade) then took the CHSPE. Now she is enrolled at a community college. *"The decision to homeschool (my parents' at the time, though my brother and I readily agreed) was based mainly on a dissatisfaction with*

*the schools available to us (both public and private).
My parents didn't feel our needs were being met,
and looking back I certainly agree. I had been to various different public and private schools during my
short career as an elementary school student, and
none were satisfactory to myself or my parents. I'm
not sure any school could have been. Children
aren't meant to sit at desks for six to seven hours a
day, and I can remember hating it."*

"Highlights?" she responds, *"There have been
so many. My parents' way of teaching us was very
unstructured, so we had a lot of time to play. That
play time is so important for children, I wouldn't
trade it for anything."*

*"I don't feel that home schooling has in any
way hampered any of my goals. I don't really see
how it could, at least not any goals I might have.
Perhaps that would differ for someone else, I don't
know. I am presently a student at both Grossmont
and Cuyamaca community colleges, and if anything
my educational background has helped, not hin-
dered me. I haven't had 12 years during which to
get burned out on school. I'm here by my own
choice."*

Besides asking in general about her home
school experiences and how they have affected her
educational opportunities, I also asked Diana what
effect her learning experience has had on her life.
Diana replied, *"One definite factor for me has been
time. My more liberal time schedule enabled me to
get a job at age 14, something I really wanted to do.
This past January marked my third year at the*

*health food store. I don't think it is bragging or ex-
aggerating to say I'm one of the more valued em-
ployees. I also feel as if home schooling helped to
enable me to relate to people on a more adult level
at an earlier age. This, however, was also affected by
the way I was treated by my parents--as an equal. I
trust my parents completely, and I was never made
to feel afraid of them. I suppose that's a difference
between me and a lot of public schooled friends I
have. I get along with my parents, I enjoy their
company and I think we have a mutual respect for
each other that isn't an every day thing."*

*"Accomplishments? Well I'm not up for any
Nobel prizes or anything. I guess my job is something I'm proud of. I think I work pretty hard--
when I do something I try to do it well. Another
thing I could mention is my grades. I began college
at age 16. This month marks the beginning of my
third semester, and so far I've kept up a 4.0 GPA. To
me that's an accomplishment because I really went
into school cold turkey--at home we never really
had a set curriculum--we did 'school work' whenever we felt like it--which wasn't very often at all
(almost never). So for me to go into college with no
study skills and little formal schooling at all and do
as well as I did is something of an accomplishment."*

Diana presented her ideas on how teachers can
most effectively teach and how parents can be effective in their children's learning experiences. *"First
and foremost, I stress that teachers have to like kids
a lot. Someone who doesn't can't really interact effectively with them. Also, they have to be teaching*

*for the right reasons--not because they like the
schedule (summers off) or because they enjoy it.
And they should enjoy what they're teaching. It
isn't fun to learn from someone who's not interested in what they're teaching. I've had teachers like
that."*

Diana adds, *"Every child is an individual and
has varied needs, so what each family does will be
different. It's hard to recommend anything without
knowing the situation. What I would stress is that
children be allowed to learn (or not learn) at their
own pace. I don't think it's necessary to be constantly providing entertainment for children, or to provide sources of educational material. There's a lot
to do in your own backyard, and children will discover that if given the opportunity."*

Ending her letter, Diana writes, *"A final note of
advice to parents is not to worry. Parents worry that
they aren't giving children enough mental stimula-
tion or that they aren't providing the necessary educational background for them to attend college. I'm
living proof that the case is otherwise, so don't worry! Just enjoy!"*

One respondent, Felice, struggled with her
studies in both the formal school setting and the unstructured setting of the School of Home Learning.
She home schooled for two high school years because *"my interests were not learning; at the time
they were more on playing around."* She lamented
that her public high school classes were so crowded
that the teachers did not realize, *"that I needed special attention, because lots of the time I didn't un-*

derstand them and then they would just go on to the next thing." She thought the highlights of her home school experience were that she could make her own time and not get up so early.

When discussing what she would do differently, Felice said, *"I think if I was in a better home schooling program, that I would have stayed with it regularly--because of that I do sort of regret not finishing regular school--because I think I would have grown to appreciate it. Yes, I do need someone to tell me 'This is due tomorrow, you have to do it now.' I didn't have that with my home school program."*

By the time she was 18, Felice had several work experiences. She worked in a store and was manager for some time. While working for a year in a Century 21 realty office, she programmed their computer. And she has worked at a medical billing office where, she says, she learned a lot.

Felice had family problems including her father's death and mother's divorce. Because of her mother's job, Felice did not see her very often. She says, *"One thing, I have had to grow up a lot faster and my parents have taught me to be real responsible. When I see my old school mates I feel like I am five years older than them--they're still stupid as ever."*

As to what she would advise teachers and parents, Felice pointed out that it is important to be aware of problems students may be facing. Also, it is important to keep things simple and to the point. *"So many teachers try to explain five things at one time."* She points out that it was her mother who burned out during the home schooling and feels that a lot depends on the program chosen. *"Be very selective!!"* Felice cautions.

The advice Felice would give to a friend who was having problems is to give it your all. Don't quit when the going gets hard, but explore all your possibilities. *"And if they are still having a hard time, try home studies. It takes a lot of discipline on the student's part, though. So be prepared and if it doesn't work out, don't quit, it may be your attitude."*

Originally I had written to Meshawn, but her younger sister saw the letter and was intrigued so she responded instead. Cheannie started home schooling as a high school freshman. *"I had no choice in this situation. My parents didn't like my attitude, my friends, or the whole school system. I loved school, did very well with my grades, and had no problem being liked."* Local drug abuse at the high school motivated her parents to remove Cheannie from school.

Once in the home school program, Cheannie began to realize the benefits of studying at her own pace. She now has set her sights on going into the fields of psychology and nutrition. *"I plan on combining the two and becoming very successful in it. One thing about home study that was always on my good side was working at your own pace. That's real helpful if you plan on going to college because, if you wish you can start your college training earlier."*

As for advice she would give a friend having

difficulties in school, Cheannie would tell them to *"consider home study if they have the initiative to learn and work hard. If a student hates school and is struggling to keep their head above water, the chance of them actually learning and enjoying something is small. And that, to me, is a waste of a precious mind."*

Earlier I told of Laurie Struble's experiences with her son, Sam, and how unstructured home schooling filled his educational needs. She shared her story of her daughter Krishanda, which illustrates the varied needs of our children.

"On to Krishanda. . .she's so different, as I mentioned before. She was a "late bloomer". I was so glad I knew about homeschooling with her, because it would have been traumatic to have had to make her go to school when she was only 5 or 6. She was very needful and was my constant companion for years. When she was 7, she started taking dance class one day a week for one hour. And I was always right outside the room. Scholastically, she just wasn't interested. She never really liked books when she was little, and wasn't must interested in learning to read. I'd read about the theories that thought early reading was detrimental. And sure enough, when she was ready, she caught up with no problem."

Laurie noticed that when Krishanda was nine she got serious about wanting to go to school. Laurie was busy with a new baby so she put her off for about six months. Finally Laurie gave in and signed her up for a Montessori school. *"I really didn't want*

*her going to school, but I knew I couldn't, in good
conscience, hold her back. It turned out beautifully.
She was ready."* After a year and a half Krishanda
begged to try public school. Despite strong misgivings Laurie felt it was important to let her "follow
her own path." That worked out well.

After Sam's terrible experience at high school,
Laurie again had misgivings as Krishanda entered
junior high. But once again it was right for Krishanda. *"She's so mature and we have a close relationship and I just couldn't ask for more. Academically she's doing great, her teachers love her. I
can see that as much as I love homeschooling, she is
where she belongs."*

CHAPTER SIX

COPING WITH PARENT - TEACHER WEAR AND TEAR

"I could never teach my youngsters at home. I could not stand being around them all day every day. Most of all, I do not have all the time necessary to teach my own youngsters. How in the world do you manage it?" Every home schooling parent has probably heard these comments many times. Some could truthfully respond that it does indeed take a great deal of preparation time besides time necessary for lesson presentation.

However, I find that I actually spend just about as much time as I did when Jim, Laurie, and Susan were in school because I was so actively involved in each of their schools. My preparation time is minimal since all three youngsters know what they want to learn and how to find their own materials. Often they inform me that they do not want my interference in the learning process.

But this does not mean that every day runs smoothly nor that there are never days I anxiously hover over them checking "progress". Some days it is impossible for them to get along with each other. There are days when learning is actively resisted. Other days are spent in nothingness. The house is in greater chaos than usual. Chores are undone because "It's not MY job!" A skateboard goes through a sliding glass door--"I didn't mean to do it! It wasn't going that fast." I am preparing a salad so reach for the vinegar only to discover just in time that the vinegar also contains baking soda because of an experiment constructing volcanoes performed without my knowledge.

There are days when I wonder if anything works. One youngster is in tears because she does not want to do her math and another has stubbornly set her face in refusal to do a writing assignment. I have reverted to my teacher role and everything seems to be wrong. Maybe I am not giving them enough or not teaching something their peers already have learned. I am not as clever as the teacher who lives down the street who does marvels in her classroom. Doubts assail me from all sides. Will they survive in college, in the world of work? Am I hurting their futures?

One day Pat tells me how happy she is when my youngsters come over to her house because they help her own youngsters' study efforts. She loves to observe them at play because my youngsters are teaching hers so much about geography and proper word usage during their play. Suddenly I realize everything is working out. I can truthfully tell Pat that I have observed the very same characteristics in her youngsters when they are at our house. Both of us gain perspective.

Pat has struggled with first using a highly structured learning program with her youngsters and nearly burning out because of her lack of confidence in herself. She has relatives who are public school administrators and very critical of home schooling. Each year Pat gains confidence and gradually gives her youngsters greater freedom in their studies. She readily admits that had she continued with the strict study schedule she started with she could not have worked very long with her youngsters. Her youngsters are much happier now and progressing rapidly from the love they have of learning.

Coping with parent - teacher wear and tear involves knowing deep down that the children will learn despite your worry and efforts. As Diana Scheck reminds parents, *"Don't worry--just enjoy. Trust your children. When they feel the need to know something, they will learn it much easier and faster when they have the freedom of choice and self-confidence."*

A Canadian friend once reminded me in a moment of doubt that even when children go off to school some place, parental responsibility does not cease. She said to look at my children and listen to them. Most of all I should listen to my heart. "Professionals" don't have all the answers in education any more than doctors know all about illness or health. It is so important to explore alternatives and to step in to change a situation that is not suitable for a given child. Beth ended by saying that no one loves my children as I do, nor understands their specialness as I do. I am their protector, spokesperson, and defender until each is able to take on the task for herself.

To prevent my own "burn out" I find I need to replace my self-doubt with trusting myself. Whenever I start setting too high expectations on myself and my children, I notice lessening ability to cope in myself. Even though I have had the advantage of extensive volunteer work in the classroom as well as my own experiences of teaching other youngsters, there are times I catch myself with an unrealistic view of what takes place in the nation's classrooms. This teacher is doing a fantastic unit on the space shuttle with her first graders, why can't I?

Susan's kindergarten teacher stressed math manipulatives while another terrific kindergarten teacher in the same school presented an in-depth study of flowers to her students. A third teacher emphasized dinosaurs and used a lot of music with her kindergarten class. There is no way in the world that every kindergarten class in the country is going to learn exactly the same things. Why should I expect myself to be all things to my students? Even on the high school level teachers will present their subjects differently from each other even if both teach social studies, science, or whatever.

My youngsters want me to be a facilitator not a dictator. They are freer to let me know what they think about something I want them to do than they are with another teacher. When they do not want to write, or whatever I want them to do, tears will flow if I pressure them too much. Learning will not take place even if my will prevails. Yet they did not do this in school because it would have been useless. Instead they did the assignment resenting every moment of it. Learning did not take place then, either.

Sometimes it requires skillful questioning to find the source of the resistance. Usually it is a result of lack of interest in the project and seeing no sense in completing it. The projects that they want to pursue by far present the best results--and often surprising ones at that.

"I'm bored!" is sometimes heard around here. But not all that often since I usually hand their boredom right back to them. I tell them that they are the only ones who can do something about the problem. There are times they really do want some suggestions from me, though, so when I sense this I offer ideas. Other times I realize that they are only saying they are bored to obtain a reaction from me. I tell them that I have yet to read of a documented case where someone actually died from boredom. At times I do scrutinize our activities to see if the boredom is a result of unsuitable activities. Boredom can be beneficial when it leads to new explorations.

I find the use of a year round flexible schedule

has its advantages in warding off burnout. It affects
me more than it does the youngsters as we don't
change our daily activities much all year around.
However, for record keeping purposes I only need to
be concerned about a nine week stretch at a time
with a four week break from record keeping. My
records are minimal but there is a psychological relief every so often. A flexible learning schedule pre-
vents cramming studies into specified days or hours
because activities taking place outside the Monday
through Friday nine to three time frames are considered of value to the learning process. So if nothing seems to happen between nine and one on
Monday, all is not lost.

I do not have to always be present for learning
to take place. Depending on the ages of your children, you do not have to be present at all times either. I find it necessary to take breaks away from the
children. When the children are older it is possible
to go off shopping or running errands while they re-
main at home. My youngsters are also a big help
with shopping and running errands. They have become skilled comparison shoppers and can handle
financial affairs with ease.

Every morning while they are preparing their
breakfasts and doing their few morning chores, I
take a brisk twenty minute walk to a nearby park.
This is my time of peace. Sometime I use it to plan
the day's activities and other times I just quietly enjoy my surroundings without much thought in particular. I call this time my sanity saver.

Because my youngsters are older, other home

schooling families ask them to baby-sit. Mothers of young children and preschoolers appreciate having Laurie or Jim around their youngsters. When the mother remains at home while Jim or Laurie is present, she feels the relief of having the youngsters occupied by someone else. Other times the mothers welcome the opportunity to run errands, etc., without small helpers.

Jim, Laurie, and Susan sometimes help their friends with their studies. This works out very well for all concerned. Mothers have free moments to themselves, students learn more readily, and student/tutors clarify their own skills.

Many areas have home school support groups. Our support group is very informal. We meet in local parks once a month to plan field trips and discuss items of interest. We also make arrangements for rental of our municipal swimming pool each week. It is important to have someone with whom you can exchange ideas. Our group serves this purpose. Some people do not seem to have as great a need for outside support. Or maybe they have other sources of support. Burnout seems to occur more often among those lacking some kind of support.

Besides our local support group, I have subscriptions to *Growing Without Schooling, Home Education Magazine, Northern California Homeschoolers Association News,* and the newsletters put out by John Boston for the *California Coalition-People for Alternative Learning Situations* and his *Home Centered Learning.* Another publication I find useful is *Learning 89.* These magazines and newsletters reinforce my belief in the value of student interest initiated learning. I am always searching for appropriate books to add to my already extensive library.

Occasionally I do begin to show signs of parent - teacher wear and tear. My first signs usually are the sensation that I am working harder, accomplishing less and feeling very tired. Then disappointment in myself and the children begins to set in along with irritability. Making one phone call or writing a letter becomes harder to do. There is less joy and I start to regard events and people negatively. The question about whether it is worth the effort begins to nag at me. This is when I need to seriously examine what is occurring in my life.

I discovered Dr. Wayne Dyer's book, What Do You Really Want For Your Children?, helps me to reassess what I am doing and why. It is almost as if he looked over my shoulder the day I put down on paper my educational goals for my children. He reaffirms my desire to impart to Jim, Laurie, and Susan the ability to enjoy life, to be risk takers, to value themselves, to handle stress, to be creative, to have a sense of purpose, and most of all to value themselves. His aim in writing his book was to offer specific suggestions to parents for assisting their youngsters to realize their full potential based on his experiences in working with troubled youngsters and families.

When preparing to present a series of classes on parenting, I found another book that I use in moments of doubt and stress. Dolores Curran wrote

Stress and the Healthy Family because in her research into what differentiates functional families
from dysfunctional families most, she found, was
the ability to handle the every day stresses that occur. She listed the top family stresses as economics,
behavior of children, lack of shared family responsi-
bilities, insufficient family and individual time, lack
of communication, and guilt for not accomplishing
more. The two important stresses most overlooked
are insufficient family playtime and over-scheduled
family calendars.

Her book shares the dramatic turnarounds
some families have made in eliminating pressures
and increasing pleasures in family life. One conclusion to her study that helps me resolve my own
doubts is that functional families seek solutions
while dysfunctional families seek blame.

A third book that I find beneficial is Adele Fa-
ber and Elaine Mazlish's How to Talk So Kids Will
Listen and Listen So Kids Will Talk. The authors
continually remind me that my youngsters are people, too. They have feelings. They have reasons for
doing what they do. I must truly listen to them.
And I need to help them express their own feelings
in a positive and accepting manner. I have had this
book for so many years and read it so often that I
now only need to glance at it's cover on a promi-
nent bookshelf during a time of frustration to remind myself that I want them to control and be responsible for their own actions. Every now and
then I have to open the book to one of the graphic
cartoons to bring perspective back into my reactions

to something the youngsters have done or failed to do.

Sometimes my concerns center more on whether I am taking the correct educational approach for my children. When this is the case, I retreat to certain favorite books and magazines which reinforce and renew my sagging spirits. I am committed to providing Jim, Laurie, and Susan with the opportunities to pursue interest initiated learning in the manner most suitable for them as individuals.

There are times I feel overwhelmed by people and literature that warn me I must control their learning because they are incapable of choosing wisely for themselves. Then I seek out other opinions with the realization that no one has yet discovered any definitive answers as to what constitutes learning and how to most effectively enhance it. The workings of the human mind are still a mystery to mankind. Therefore I have to discover the philosophy of education with which I am most comfortable and then act accordingly.

My teacher training background emphasized classroom management more than it did subject content or how learning occurs. When Jim had his problems in middle school I became more acutely aware of the learning environment. I had already read David Elkind's excellent books, The Hurried Child, and All Grown Up and No Place to Go. He deplored the stresses to succeed our young people are put under in the educational system and from parents. In his more recent book. Miseducation, he is even more worried about the harmful effects of the move to push academics on preschoolers.

In Miseducation Dr. Elkind cites a study of gifted and talented people conducted by Benjamin Bloom and his colleagues of 120 talented and successful people. The parents of these eminent people did not impose their own priorities on their children but chose to follow each child's lead. The most important factor was the excitement and enthusiasm for learning. Skills were easily learned when there was motivation.

Dr. Helen K. Billings planted the seeds of doubt in my mind as to the effectiveness of most schooling. At a conference on parenting in 1976, I had the privilege of introducing Dr. Billings during the session she was to present on giving your child an educational advantage. In preparation for my introduction she and I had a lively conversation. She impressed me with the importance of following a child's interests. Because at the time I only had preschoolers I only applied what she said to preschoolers. Now I realize she meant all children, regardless of age.

Her professional career went from teaching in a one room country school to head of the Department of Education at the college level. She founded the Montessori Institute of America. While Advisor on Academic Affairs for Southeastern University she developed a masters program in child development designed to apply the philosophy of independent study to higher education.

Dr. Billings believed that student initiated

learning is the basis for true education. In her books she insisted that learning cannot be carried on solely within the walls of a classroom. The child best learns about life by living it within the community. The student needs the freedom to learn on her own with the adult standing by to answer questions or to guide when asked.

I read a reprint of a 1952 article by Carl Rogers entitled "Personal Thoughts on Teaching and Learning" in which he laments ever telling someone how to teach. He had come to the conclusion that only a self-discovered, self-appropriated learning influences behavior. He found that the results of his teaching seemed to cause the student to distrust her own experience and stifled significant learning. He was relieved when he discovered that the Danish philosopher, Soren Kierkegaard, had come to a similar conclusion. The implication appropriated and assimilated through experience is the basis for all effective learning.

The many books written by John Holt as well as his bimonthly newsletter *Growing Without Schooling* were the catalyst that caused me to find out as much information as I could about the effectiveness of interest initiated learning. I find myself referring constantly to one of his books or back issues of his newsletter. He insisted that most of what he knew he did not learn in school and was not even "taught". Between 1964 and 1983 he wrote eleven books on how people learn most effectively. In one of his last articles before his death, he observes that the less unasked for corrections the student experiences the better the results of the learning process. Children need time to find their own way.

In Teach Your Own John Holt warns against parents trying to make the home more of a school than school itself is. He argues that this is the fastest way to burn out. Many home schooling parents start out trying to know too much, to do too much, and control too much. My own youngsters do not hesitate to let me know when I fall into that trap. Thank goodness, because it is when I am inappropriately trying too hard that I am most susceptible to burnout.

Dr. Raymond Moore is a developmental psychologist whose research on the family and school has appeared in nearly every academic journal in the field of education in the United States. He is the founder and director of The Moore Foundation. Along with his wife, Dorothy, who is a reading specialist, Dr. Moore has co-authored several books on the benefits of home schooling.

In their book, Home Grown Kids, they introduce parents to the idea that they can provide a first-class education in the home environment that enhances creativity and character development. The focus of the book is from birth to about the age of nine. Home Spun Schools presents case histories of home schooling parents. They demonstrate that one-on-one teaching is more effective for learning than crowded classrooms. In their third book in this series, Home Style Teaching, the Moores present practical insights into the art and science of teaching. Addressing the issue of socialization, they assert that while learning at home the youngsters experience relative quiet and simplicity in schedule, thereby attaining a sense of personal worth. Then when the child does interact socially with greater numbers of people, she is already confident and independent in thinking and values. There is not the negative peer pressure to affect actions.

During a home school conference, I listened as Raymond Moore gave a presentation where he stressed the necessity of letting youngsters learn according to their particular interests. He cited numbers of instances where he knew parents had given up working with their children at home because of burn out caused by "schooling at home" rather than "home schooling." He referred to families that expected far more than the school systems expect of their students. The families most prone to burnout are those who cram learning down their children without regard for the abilities and interests of the students.

Dr. Moore says that the more formally the parents approach home schooling the higher the rate of burnout. Those families who persevere are the ones who come to recognize the true educational need of their children to pursue learning in a more relaxed manner according to their interests.

In order to concentrate on working with my youngsters, my husband and I have chosen to be part of John Boston's Home Centered Learning because he emphasizes the benefits of student interest initiated learning. This psychologically frees me to focus on my educational goals without unnecessary worry over administrative details. However, I consider it my responsibility to keep abreast of legal concerns for home schoolers.

Other parents, where available, choose to participate in their public school district's Independent Study Program for the same reason. However, in some cases the local Independent Study programs have not worked in the children's best interests. Many other parents I know choose to file their own private school affidavits according to California's present educational code. Different, acceptable, alternatives exist. Each family can choose what works best for them.

How each family reacts to parent - teacher wear and tear determines how successful they will be in home schooling. For me it has been necessary to reassess my firm belief in the value of interest initiated learning and the goals I have for myself and my family.

Sometimes I do this by reviewing how I have struggled this past year to learn how to use a computer and a word processor. This has given me renewed appreciation of how important it is to be interested in a subject to learn it effectively. Laurie has quickly mastered using a desk top publishing program because she uses it to put out her monthly newsletter. I've struggled to use it the few times I've wanted to do work on a newsletter.

I have recognized the value of my claiming personal time for myself to pursue my interests. And I know that I need the periodic support that my friends provide. Most of all my youngsters have taught me that they indeed can be trusted to select what is of importance for them to learn. They will learn when they are ready and when they see a purpose to knowing something. These are my ways of coping with parent - teach wear and tear.

CONCLUSION

Interest initiated learning is that learning which the learner herself controls and initiates according to her interests. When it is interest initiated, learning is guided by internal personal priorities not imposed from the outside. The learner herself chooses when and how to learn about a given topic or skill. It is entirely self-directed. The teacher only enters into the learning process when invited to do so.

Most learning is unmeasurable. Close observers of how learning takes place in students who are self-directed note that ideas will gestate for some time, even months, and then reappear in more mature form than when first introduced. Standardized tests are unable to measure the learning that has taken place during periods of seemingly unproductive periods of daydreaming.

John Holt stated that it is better for a child to figure out something on her own than to be told what to do. She will then remember better and she will gain confidence in her ability to figure things out. When we try to measure the knowledge gained we undermine the learner's self-confidence. To

John Holt, testing was detrimental to the success of interest initiated learning.

He felt that too often teachers and parents believe that learning only happens in children when the adults make it happen. Because children have to be in school and have to do what they're told, many teachers rarely get reliable feedback from the students they are teaching. People who teach their own children at home are likely to quickly become effective teachers because they receive unmistakable feedback from the children that tells them when the teaching is helpful and when it is not.

Because many American educators did not listen to what he had to say about the value of interest initiated learning, John Holt turned to the first teachers of children, parents. He devoted his later years to developing the theory of the importance of interest initiated learning. He firmly believed that the amount a person can learn at a given moment depends on how she feels about her ability to do the task. Most of all, he emphasized, adults must overcome distrust of the learning capacity of children and the desire to control children.

It was largely because of the influence John Holt had on me when I decided to home school my children that I become interested in the concept of interest initiated learning. Friends pointed out to me that I already had been practicing interest initiated learning with my own children from the time of birth.

My mentor, Dr. Joanne Deaton, in my Master's program with Columbia Pacific University prompted my writing this book when she suggested that others could profit from my experiences with implementing interest initiated learning. I thought that the experiences of other families who practice student interest initiated learning would enhance the book.

There are many theories relating to education prevalent today. The more popular ones seem to emphasize adult control and the necessity for an "expert" to direct learning activities. We have a nation that believes in freedom of choice and equality in differences. Yet there are those in power who prefer conformity and uniformity that disregards the needs of the individual.

Christopher Hurn devotes his entire textbook, The Limits and Possibilities of Schooling: An Introduction to the Sociology of Education, to the conflicting theories on the purpose of our schools and how learning should be implemented in them. In his conclusion he comments that the compulsory character of schooling, crowded conditions, and lack of incentive to learn are all constraints not likely to be easily removed. Because of a loss of faith in schooling as a panacea for social ills many see formal education as nothing more than a rationing of jobs or a credentialing device. If we wish to make our schools better, we must first learn more about how learning takes place and how to implement this knowledge in our schools.

California's Legislature mandated the establishment of a Self-Esteem Task Force to come up with a working definition of self-esteem. The Task Force is to seek ways to promote self-esteem with personal and social responsibility among the citizens of the state. In their publication *Esteem* they reprinted an article from *For Instructors Only*, published by Performance Learning Systems in New Jersey. The article, "School: Builder or Destroyer of Esteem?", reported that eighty percent of students entering school feel good about themselves. By fifth grade only twenty percent of the students feel good about themselves. They claim that by twelfth grade the student has received only 4,000 positive statements and about 15,000 negative statements. In all, this comes to the equivalent of sixty days each year of reprimands, nagging, and punishment. The teachers control the environment in which the student spends more than 1,000 hours a year.

One of my goals in the education of my children is that each of them will have a healthy self-esteem. After lengthy deliberation the California Task Force to Promote Self-Esteem, and Personal and Social Responsibility, decided on a definition of self-esteem that clearly states my own understanding of self-esteem: "Appreciating my own worth and importance, and having the character to be accountable for myself, and to act responsibly toward others."

Practicing interest initiated learning can only enhance the student's self-esteem. She is in control of the learning process and thereby recognizes her individual worth. She is not subjected to countless negative reactions to what she is accomplishing.

I watched my own son restore his self-esteem

when he experienced interest initiated learning. Although he has chosen to return to the school system, I see him controlling his own life and studies because he values his own judgement.

I am watching a daughter who was beginning to lose her sense of self-worth while in first grade. She was in a classroom that allowed more student initiative than most classrooms in our school district. She is now showing me daily that she does understand her capabilities and how to put them to the best use. I have no doubts that she is a much better judge of when she is ready to proceed in her learning experiences than I am. At the age of nine she has an understanding of math that I will never attain.

Our other daughter delights in being around people. She knows characteristics of every subscriber on her newspaper route and receives generous tips from her appreciative customers. Her contacts reach over the Pacific Ocean with a long time pen pal in Australia and another one in Japan. Her Campfire leader relies on her to organize many of their activities. Because of her our family rarely has dull moments. She flourishes when she directs her learning activities.

Not every person is suited to interest initiated learning as a means of education. In my observation, the longer a student is exposed to other-directed and controlled learning, the harder it is to adapt to interest initiated learning. John Boston, Raymond Moore, and John Holt have also made this observation. Many students (adult students in-

cluded) depend upon being told what to do and how
to do it.

When I told a neighbor I was completing my
college degree work through independent study projects she asked to borrow my brochures on the program because she is completing college requirements after raising her family. A week later she
returned the materials ruefully commenting that
she could never do it as she needs someone to tell
her what to study.

In talking with other home schooling families
locally and at conferences, it is evident that the older
the student is when starting home study, the more
difficult it is for her to adjust. Of the alumni from
the Home Centered Learning who answered my letter, those who began the program earlier were more
likely to continue through high school.

Entering school after home schooling does not
seem to present many problems. There may be a
few problems with daily routine at first, but most
youngsters quickly master them. My cousin's husband teaches fifth grade. A girl enrolled in his class
after home schooling for all her academic life. To
his delight he found that he wished he had more
students like her because she was so enthusiastic
about learning and was self-directed.

My friend, Lauri Struble, commented, "As to
the question of entering school after home schooling, I can't see that it's any problem. If the kids
WANT to go, they'll do fine. Sam is finally getting
serious about starting college, but it took him awhile
after passing the CHSPE. I think most people as-

sume homeschooled kids will be eager to go to college as soon as they're old enough, but I don't see why. Sam learns so well at home and enjoys it so much, there's really no hurry." Her daughter, Krishanda certainly had no problems with entering school when she chose to after completely interest initiated learning at home.

In summary, interest initiated learning is that learning which the learner herself initiates according to her interests. She is guided by her own priorities not by those imposed from outside. The teacher only enters into the learning process when invited to do so by the student. In choosing our learning materials, my youngsters prove to me that it is possible for children to make better sense of the world on their own than adults can through adult produced curricula.

The student needs both time and opportunity to reflect on the barrage of information to which she is exposed. Her learning rhythms of advance and retreat, exploration and consolidation cannot be predicted or controlled.

Trust is the key to success in interest initiated learning. Interest initiated learning allows the student to use her abilities in the optimal manner. The amount she can learn at a given moment depends on how she feels about her ability to do the task. "Control" seems to be the reason that some adults have problems with accepting the idea that children learn much more through interest initiated learning rather than through other-directed learning. Until we accept that the human mind remains a mystery, we operate under the delusion that it is possible to measure and control what goes on in students' minds.

A student needs to discover on her own what contributions she wants to make to society in an atmosphere that promotes excitement for learning all that she can. Long term enthusiasm for learning is a result of allowing the student to set her own learning priorities and pace in a supportive, non-pressured environment.

SELECTED RESOURCES

BOOKS

Alternatives in Education, The Home School Reader
Both published by Home Education Press, PO Box 1083, Tonasket, WA 98855; (509) 486-1351 (*Alternatives In Education* was substantially revised in 1993).
Homeschooling For Excellence
Published by Warner Books, available from Mountain House Books, PO Box 353, Philo, CA 95466
Home Grown Kids, Home Spun Schools, Home Style Teaching
Available from Moore Foundation, Box 1, Washougal, WA 98607; (206) 835-2736

MAGAZINES

Home Education Magazine, PO Box 1083, Tonasket, WA 98855; (509) 486-1351 - bimonthly, $24.00 per year, $4.50 current issue, free 24 page books and publications catalog
Growing Without Schooling, 2269 Massachusetts Ave, Cambridge, MA 02140; (617) 864-3100 - bimonthly, $25.00 per year, $4.50, free 24 page books and publications catalog
KidsArt, PO Box 274, Mt. Shasta, CA 96067; (916) 926-5076; (800) 959-5076 - quarterly, $8.00
Ranger Rick, National Wilflife Federation, 1400 Sixteenth St., Washington, DC 20078-6420; (800) 432-6564 - monthly, $15.00
Zillions, PO Box 54861, Boulder, CO 80322-4861; (800) 234-2078 - bimonthly, $16.00

CATALOGS

Aristoplay, PO Box 7529, Ann Arbor, MI 48107; (800) 634-7738
The National Center for Fair and Open Testing (Fairtest), 342 Broadway, Cambridge, MA 02139; (617) 864-4810
TOPS Science Learning Systems, 10970 S. Mulino Rd, Canby, OR 97013

MISCELLANEOUS

Clonlara School, 1289 Jewett St., Ann Arbor, MI 48104; (313) 769-4515
Home Centered Learning, PO Box 4643, Whittier, CA 90607; (310) 696-4696
National Coalition of Alternative Community Schools (NCACS), PO Box 15036, Santa Fe, NM 87506; (505) 474-4312
Washington Homeschool Research Project, Jon Wartes, 16109 NE 169th Place, Woodinville, WA 98072
World Almaniac Contest, PO Box 53, La Canada, CA 91011

INDEX